Christian Mindfulness

Books by Peter Tyler

The Way of Ecstasy: Praying with St Teresa of Avila

Confession: The Healing of the Soul

*The Pursuit of the Soul: Psychoanalysis, Soul-making
and the Christian Tradition*

Teresa of Avila: Doctor of the Soul

*The Return to the Mystical: Ludwig Wittgenstein, Teresa of Avila
and the Western Mystical Tradition*

St John of the Cross: Outstanding Christian Thinker

*Picturing the Soul: Revisioning Psychotherapy
and Spiritual Direction*

The Bloomsbury Guide to Christian Spirituality
(with Richard Woods)

Mystical Theology: Renewing the Contemplative Tradition
(with Chris Cook and Julienne McLean)

*Teresa of Avila: Mystical Theology and Spirituality
in the Carmelite Tradition*
(with Edward Howells)

Sources of Transformation: Revitalizing Christian Spirituality
(with Edward Howells)

Christian Mindfulness

Theology and Practice

Peter Tyler

scm press

© Peter Tyler 2018

Published in 2018 by SCM Press
Editorial office
3rd Floor, Invicta House,
108–114 Golden Lane,
London EC1Y 0TG, UK

www.scmpress.co.uk

SCM Press is an imprint of Hymns Ancient & Modern Ltd
(a registered charity)

Hymns Ancient & Modern® is a registered trademark of
Hymns Ancient & Modern Ltd

13A Hellesdon Park Road, Norwich,
Norfolk NR6 5DR, UK

All rights reserved. No part of this publication may be reproduced,
stored in a retrieval system, or transmitted,
in any form or by any means, electronic, mechanical,
photocopying or otherwise, without the prior permission of
the publisher, SCM Press.

The Author has asserted his right under the Copyright, Designs and
Patents Act 1988 to be identified as the Author of this Work

British Library Cataloguing in Publication data

A catalogue record for this book is available
from the British Library

978 0 334 05671 3

Typeset by Regent Typesetting Ltd
Printed and bound by
CPI Group (UK) Ltd

Contents

A Prologue Out of Silence   vii
Abbreviations   xi

1. Mindfulness or Heartfulness?   1
2. The Mindful Psychology of the Desert   17
3. The Iberian School of Mindfulness and Mental Prayer   39
4. The Mindful Way – St Teresa of Avila and St John of the Cross   61
5. Thomas Merton – Mindful Clarity of Heart   92
6. Living a Mindful Life – The Indian Tradition   123

Epilogue   151
Acknowledgements   157
Bibliography   159
Index of Names and Subjects   167

A Prologue Out of Silence

The answer is within you. Seek it in the depths of your being. Devote yourself to meditation and the solution will be given you.[1]

Silence is the language of God, all the rest is bad translation.[2]

All prayer emerges out of silence and returns to silence – the abyss of silence that Christians call 'the Father'. One of the first Christians, St Paul, described it thus:

> The spirit participates in our weakness for we do not know how to pray as we should,
> But that very Spirit supplicates on our behalf with unutterable groanings.
>
> And the Father who searches the heart knows the mind of the Spirit,
> Because the Spirit intercedes for the saints according to God.
> We know that in all things God works for good for those who love God
> And they are called according to God's purpose.
> And for those whom he knew long ago
> He also destined that they be conformed to the Ikon of his Son
> So that He would be the first-born of a large family.
> (Letter to the Romans 8.26–29)

Throughout this book I shall return to these words of St Paul and what we shall refer to as the Trinitarian shape of Christian prayer.

Twenty years ago Christine Smith of Canterbury Press and Bishop Graham Chadwick commissioned my first published book: *The Way of Ecstasy: Praying with St Teresa of Avila*. In the intervening years, which seems like a lifetime, two major things have happened that now compel me to return some decades later to the ground covered in the earlier book. First, and unsurprisingly, has been the natural ageing process. The middle-aged man in his mid-fifties is not the 'ever questing youth' who wrote the first book. In the meantime, my first-born has been joined by 11 brothers and sisters, a doctorate in mystical theology, degrees in psychotherapy and a chair in pastoral theology. The joy of exploring the mystical tradition in the academic setting is unending and cannot be overestimated. However, over the years many readers have asked me to write something simpler, more straightforward, something in the spirit of *The Way of Ecstasy*. Time, and other commitments, have not allowed this to happen – until now. So when SCM Press bravely approached me again for a new work I thought of suggesting something in the spirit of *Ecstasy* but that also reflected the new development that has arisen since that earlier book was written – what we usually refer to nowadays as 'the mindfulness revolution'. Just as a great wave of 'spirituality' hit us towards the end of the last millennium, so now we find ourselves again, in this new age of uncertainty, at a high tide of mindfulness.

Many commentators, not least Christian commentators, have been taken aback by the seemingly unstoppable rise of the 'mindfulness revolution' that has swept the country over the past decade.[3] What is striking looking back at *The Way of Ecstasy* is how much of what is accepted as mainstream practice now was then introduced as new or innovative. I recall disagreements with readers over issues that today would now be completely commonplace.

Accordingly, in this new book I aim to reflect on the nature of mindfulness, especially as perceived from its Buddhist roots (as currently operative on the present Anglophone scene),[4] and how this may (or may not) relate to the wider tradition of Christian prayer. I shall argue that far from a foreign import, mindfulness is not only endemic but essential to the Christian understanding of how the human person relates to the divine. This will be the 'theology' that is presented here.

However, before we begin, I would like to add some caveats to the basic position of this book – that mindfulness is good for you. One thing that does disturb some Christian souls (and a cursory glance at the internet will confirm this) is how far can mindfulness be seen as a covert import from Buddhism and how far are Christians adopting Buddhist techniques, ideas and ideologies. This is not an unimportant consideration. Similar issues have troubled Christians over the past few decades as successive waves of Eastern wisdom have dashed themselves against the Western fortresses of Christendom: transcendental meditation in the 1970s, yoga in the 1980s and 1990s and now, the latest arrival, mindfulness. Perhaps their cumulative effect is to weaken the foundations of Christianity, yet during my travels in India I have encountered thousands of Christians who employ meditation and yoga as part of their daily Christian practice (as their communities have done so for years if not centuries) while not showing themselves thereby to be somehow weakened in their Christian endeavour and mission. I shall return to their experiences in a later chapter. Yet, as other scholars have shown recently, such as Professor Gavin D'Costa in Bristol and Fr Martin Ganeri OP in Oxford, there *are* conceptual and ideological difficulties in squaring Buddhist ideology and approaches to fit the Christian circle and I think it would be intellectually naive to ignore these – something I do not intend to do here.

To begin with, then, I shall turn to the practice of mindfulness in its Buddhist origins before reflecting on its current use in healthcare, psychiatry and so on. I shall then turn to the Christian tradition of prayer before concluding with some possible future models for Christian mindfulness today.

However, as I thought more about the shape of this book I felt that due to the nature of the subject there had to be, like its predecessor of 20 years ago, practical exercises to ground the discussion and allow the reader to engage with mindfulness in an embodied fashion, not just from a theoretical perspective. Accordingly, as in my earlier book, I shall conclude each chapter with a short practical exercise for the reader. You are of course more than welcome to ignore these and continue with the theoretical discussion of the issues. However, even if you are a seasoned 'pray-er' or practitioner of mindfulness, I urge you to take a few minutes at the conclusion of each chapter to engage with the exercises, or at least reflect quietly on the issues the chapter has raised for you. I believe this will not only enhance your enjoyment of the text but allow the dialogue I am creating here, between Buddhism, Christianity and contemporary mindfulness, to take root in your soul and heart.

Finally, another innovation I will add to the present text is a series of contemplative poems that I have completed over the past two decades. As my poetical gifts are somewhat limited I hesitate to inflict them on the patient reader. However, in my last two books on the soul, of which the present volume forms a conclusion, I have stressed the importance of poetry in talking about the movements of the soul. Initially I hesitated about whether to add my own lines to head each chapter, but foolishness ultimately won over. I hope you will forgive this one indulgence on behalf of the author and perhaps, who knows, they may convey as well as the exercises and prose something of that illusive 'subtle nothingness' that is mindful contemplation.

London
Easter 2018

Notes

1 Sri Gnānānanda, quoted in Abhishiktananda 1974, p. 25.
2 Thomas Keating, in Keating 2017, p. 4.
3 I adopt the phrase from Barry Boyce, *The Mindfulness Revolution*.
4 Recent visits to Hispanophone, Francophone and Germanophone lands, where I have presented lectures on the topic, suggest something similar is occurring, albeit on a smaller scale.

Abbreviations

A   *Ascent of Mount Carmel* (St John of the Cross).
CE *The Way of Perfection* (Escorial version) (Teresa of Avila).
CV *The Way of Perfection* (Valladolid version) (Teresa of Avila).
DN *Dark Night of the Soul* (St John of the Cross).
DS *Dictionnaire de Spiritualité: Ascétique et Mystique Doctrine et Histoire*. Eds M. Viller, F. Cavallera, J. de Guibert, A. Rayez, A. Derville, P. Lamarche, A. Solignac. 1937–97. Paris: Beauchesne.
ICS Institute of Carmelite Studies, Washington.
SC *Sources Chrétiennes*, Éditions du Cerf, Paris.

I

Mindfulness or Heartfulness?

The Robin

I have a wise master
In these thin winter days.
Each morning, each evening
He accompanies my prayers –
Sifting through his precious pearls.
Attending to each
We thread them together,
My Master and I,
In a delicate web of piping sound.
His songs welcome me
In these thin winter days.
My ghostly companion
Who blesses when we understand.[1]

We seem to be in the midst of a mindfulness storm.

Until very recently comparatively few people, apart from a few dedicated practitioners, had heard of this form of meditation. Yet today there seem very few areas of healthcare, psychological intervention, education or even business and commerce that have not in some way been touched by what has been termed 'the mindfulness revolution'. Why this should be so is anyone's guess but the trend, especially in the older Western democracies, for formal religious belonging to be replaced by looser forms of spiritual expression, as traced by sociologists of religion such as Linda Woodhead and Paul Heelas, seems by now well documented and well entrenched (see, among others, Heelas and Woodhead 2004; Bullivant 2013). That this is related to the coming era of 'mindfulness' is no doubt linked.

When the molecular biologist Jon Kabat-Zinn first developed

his mindfulness courses at the University of Massachusetts in the late 1970s he was not so concerned with the metaphysical implications of what were originally Buddhist meditation practices as their clinical and medical efficacy. This novel notion of giving mindfulness meditation a sound clinical and experimental basis is what proved the essential catalyst for the subsequent explosion of mindfulness (see Boyce 2011, pp. xii–xiii). Thirty years later the clinical evidence for the efficacy of these methods in treating illnesses as diverse as depression, cancer and eating disorders is overwhelming (even though latterly there is the inevitable counter-movement expressing the 'dangers' inherent in mindfulness). This, alongside courses such as Kabat-Zinn's own Mindfulness-Based Stress Reduction programme (MBSR) – the eight-week forerunner for many of the later mindfulness courses – and the Mindfulness Based Cognitive Therapy (MBCT) developed at Oxford by Professor Mark Williams and colleagues, have contributed to the success of mindfulness as we know it today.

Kabat-Zinn himself defines mindfulness as 'paying attention in a particular way: on purpose, in the present moment, and non-judgementally' (Kabat-Zinn 1994, p. 4). This 'bare' definition is supplemented by many practitioners with wider values drawing upon something closer to traditional Buddhist notions of mindfulness. Thus Chozen Bays (2011, p. 3) suggests that it is 'deliberately paying attention, being fully aware of what is happening both inside yourself – in your body, heart and mind – and outside yourself in the environment ... it is awareness without judgement or criticism'. She goes further to state that 'when we are mindful, we are not comparing or judging. We are simply witnessing the many sensations, thoughts and emotions that come up as we engage in the ordinary activities of daily life.' We could continue multiplying these varying definitions, but – following Mace – what becomes clear when we analyse these contemporary understandings of mindfulness is that there seem to be two directions in current usage (see Mace 2008). First, the desire, as Mace himself puts it, to concentrate on the 'bare attention' – to observe, Buddha-like, the passing show of sensations, thoughts and emotion with no sticky entanglement. As neuro-biologists and scientists have become interested in the subject this 'pure bare mindfulness' (difficult as it is to isolate) has become the main source of their study. On the other hand, writers such as Chozen Bays above or Shapiro (Shapiro and Walsh 2006) link the practice with wider connotations of 'heartfulness', compassion and the general teleological development of character.

Esoteric though these debates may sound, I think they go right to the heart of the subject we shall be considering in this book: 'How far, if at all, can mindfulness be accommodated into an established religious practice such as Christianity?' And I think the answer will be (in typical philosophical fashion): 'It depends what sort of mindfulness you are talking about.' Let me explain further.

Mace makes the point that Kabat-Zinn's original 1990s formulation of the basic notion of mindfulness as commonly used today has 'something of the spirit of the US Founding Fathers' in that he wanted 'to make mindfulness available without any requirement to accept or reject particular religious beliefs' (Mace 2008, p. 59). And there can be no doubt that this agnostic method assuming no adherence to any particular religious belief system (as expounded by Kabat-Zinn and others) has clearly filled a hole in the collective psyche that was left when the box 'no religion' was ticked in numerous surveys, censuses and questionnaires (see Bullivant 2013).

The sceptical outlook of the Buddha himself – he always advised his followers not to trust his teachings but to test them and scrape them (like a goldsmith) to see if they were counterfeit – adds to their ability to fit into the prevailing *zeitgeist* of sceptical humanism within which we find ourselves. As Mace puts it, 'part of the genius of Buddhism has been to link aspects of spiritual attainment with psychological changes that can be expressed in cognitive terms. This has made it appealing to people in the West who are respectful of reason, and who believe in human potential, but distrust deist religions' (Mace 2008, p. 161).

So faced with the question, 'How far, if at all, can mindfulness be accommodated into an established religious practice such as Christianity?', as well as asking ourselves what concept of mindfulness we are applying we also need to ask a more fundamental question – what concept of religion are we applying to ourselves? Indeed, a similar question might arise for any practitioner of mindfulness whether they consider themselves a Muslim, Jew or Sikh as they came to terms with the implications of the practice for their own religion.

Training in mindfulness

My own encounter with mindfulness practices began 30 years ago when I was an idealistic young man training for the Catholic priesthood with the Society of Jesus (normally called 'the Jesuits') in the English Midlands. Our enlightened novice-master, the saintly Ian Tomlinson SJ, allowed a group of us to attend evening classes at the nearby Selly Oak Colleges of Birmingham University where we could study other religions. Although this is fairly mainstream today, this was still considered somewhat daring at the time; but Birmingham, where we were based, with its multi-ethnic and multi-cultural milieu, provided an ideal base for such an exploration. The course, initiated by the late Sr Mary Hall, included a survey of all the major world religions and it was here that I met for the first time Fuengsilapa Sarayutpilag, a diminutive Thai lay Buddhist practitioner who was married to an Englishman and known as Fuengsin Trafford. Born in 1936 in Thailand, she moved to England in the early 1960s to take up a UNESCO fellowship programme at the Institute of Education in London (she was a very skilful teacher) where she met and married her husband, Tony Trafford, a Roman Catholic who worked for HM Customs and Revenue. As her son, Paul Trafford, writes:

Brought up as a practising Buddhist, at around the age of twenty she investigated many temples in and around Bangkok for a meditation teacher. After much searching, she found a suitable teacher named Ajahn Gaew, who taught her the practice of Dhammakaya meditation. A few years later, on the day of her departure to a land far away, a large band of monks, as well as friends and colleagues, gathered at Donmuang Airport. In her tribute to Ajahn Gaew, a contribution to a memorial of his life, she relates how he informed her that she would spread the *Dhamma* in the West.[2] She found this hard to believe, but she was soon gaining experiences in Hampshire and ten to fifteen years later there were developments that made her reflect that the prediction might come true after all. (Trafford 2016)

As a pioneer in the UK she helped create the contemporary Buddhist scene by establishing and helping to form Buddhist groups across the country. As a lay-woman she was always diffident about her ability to teach the *Dhamma*; however, several abbots and teachers in Thailand gave her special permission to convey it, which she duly did before her untimely death in 1995 of cancer. Buddhism, like Christianity (or psychotherapy for that matter), is sometimes riven with disagreements and arguments between the different schools or 'vehicles'. One of Fuengsin's most endearing qualities was her ability to transcend these divisions. For her the Buddha (and Buddhism) was greater than any particular sect, and in her teachings she often went to the heart of the matter. The following quotes, collected by her son and placed on his Fuengsin website (http://fuengsin.org), which she gave in an interview to a local newspaper, give a flavour of her approach to the *Dhamma*:

> Buddhism is all about trying your best – it's not necessary to crave for perfection, because if you try too hard for anything you don't achieve it.
> When you meditate you become single-minded – that

doesn't mean narrow-minded, merely that your mind is opening up and you are more capable of appreciating and understanding things.

The key words are compassion, kindness and love.

Buddhism can change your life if you follow it – it has certainly given me strength to cope with things over the years. Based on the four [noble] truths of Buddha, life certainly becomes richer. (Trafford 2016)

Thus it was that I met this remarkable teacher while still training for the Catholic priesthood and the highlight of the course for me became Fuengsin's teaching. I had had an on-off relationship with Buddhism for many years and, as well as reading widely around the subject, I had visited Buddhist *viharas* such as the Friends of the Western Buddhist Order (now Triratna) in Bethnal Green. Fuengsin, however, was the first Eastern Buddhist I had encountered at close quarters who was able to answer (or at least try to answer) some of the many questions I had about Buddhism. She dealt with my (what were probably very stupid) questions admirably. But we also struck up a deal. For my private Buddhist tuition I would teach her Western philosophy which I had studied at Oxford University. I was very happy to do this and we found all sorts of resonances between philosophers such as Kant, Hume and Wittgenstein and the teachings of Lord Buddha. Our conversations continued for over two years, at the end of which I had decided that the Jesuit life was not for me. However, even after I had left the Order, Fuengsin and I continued to meet and debate. During this difficult part of my life she was a great source of pastoral care as well as an intellectual help – she very much embodied the practices she taught so well. I remember very vividly an occasion during this time when I asked her if I should consider taking refuge as a Buddhist. Her reply, quick as a flash, was pure Fuengsin: 'Best way for you to be Buddhist is to be a good Roman Catholic.' Wow! Here was a woman 'sent to the West' to spread the *Dhamma* urging me to remain a Roman Catholic

Christian! She was of course right as the subsequent decades have shown. I think what I sought in Buddhism then – especially mindfulness and contemplation – can be found equally upon the Christian path.

When asked to write this book I was delighted to accept and perhaps tease out again some of those wonderful synergies between Buddhism and Christianity that Fuengsin had first revealed to me. In the words of Francis Vineeth CMI, to whom we shall return later, Lord Jesus remains my 'sad-guru' – my highest guru. However, I have enormous respect also for the teachings of Lord Buddha who offers extraordinary insights into the human condition. Therefore, my hope for the book will be that it will continue the work for dialogue and harmony between the religions, very much in the loving spirit of Fuengsin and the teachings of the Catholic Church since the ground-breaking decree of the Second Vatican Council in 1965, *Nostra aetate*.

Consequently, an important part of this book will be the bringing together into dialogue of the two great faith traditions of Christianity and Buddhism. Yet, as already indicated, the present practices that go under the label of 'mindfulness' also transcend their origins in a particular world religion and seem to have developed a life of their own. With this in mind we shall need also to be aware of the fact that mindfulness as presently practised may not be what it claims to be in its Buddhist origins. For we seem to be at the birth of a new practice that seems adapted to the needs of the madly turning contemporary world.[3] I have already alluded to the varying interpretations of 'mindfulness' among contemporary commentators, and before we set out on our journey of mindfulness within the Christian tradition it may be worth spending a little more time investigating the roots of mindfulness in its Buddhist sources before turning to the contemporary interpretation of the same.

Buddhist mindfulness – its origins and purpose

As the discourse of mindfulness has developed in contemporary healthcare, psychological and educational settings there has been a tendency to draw on non-Western, especially Buddhist, sources. In this respect, when reference is made to 'mindfulness' in the Buddhist tradition, writers are usually referring to *sati*, an Indic term from the Pāli for which there is no straightforward or simple definition. The term was first translated into English as 'mindfulness' by Thomas William Rhys Davids in 1881 (Rhys Davids 1881, p. 107),[4] who noted that: '*Sati* is literally "memory" but is used with reference to the constantly repeated phrase "mindful and thoughtful" (*sato sampagāno*); and means that activity of mind and constant presence of mind which is one of the duties most frequently inculcated on the good Buddhist' (p. 145).[5]

The equivalent term in the Sanskrit canon is *smṛti* which literally means 'that which is remembered'. In the *Satipaṭṭhāna Sutta*, *sati* is paired with two other qualities. First, *sampajāna* – clearly comprehending (from the noun *sampajañña*) – which is seen as complementing the condition of mindfulness, and second, *ātāpi* or ardency: 'being intent on what you're doing, trying your best to do it skillfully' (Thanissaro Bhikku 2010, p. 2). From all three together – mindfulness, clear comprehension and ardency – we aspire to *yoniso manisikāra* or 'appropriate attention'. The term 'appropriate' is apposite as, the Buddha suggests, it precludes useless metaphysical wandering of the mind into questions such as, 'Is there a self?'

The term *ātāpi* is cognate with the Sanskrit *tapas* and suggests the conscientious effort that must accompany mindfulness; in this respect, mindfulness is not seen as a passive quality. Anālayo comments that 'applying these nuances (of *ātāpi*) to *sati*, to be "diligent" then amounts to keeping up one's contemplation with balanced but dedicated continuity, returning to the object of meditation as soon as it is lost' (2003, p. 38). *Sampajāna*, on the other hand, is cognate with the Sanskrit *sam* (joined together with) and *prajānāti* (knowing), thus giving the seeker the intense knowing that will lead to wisdom, *paññā*. Bhikku Bodhi distinguishes *sati* from *sampajañña* by suggesting that the latter allows the practitioner to clearly comprehend 'the nature and qualities of arisen phenomena and relates them to the framework defined by the parameters of the *Dhamma*, the teaching as an organic whole' (2011, p. 22). As many commentators have noted, the cognate resonance of *sati* with the Sanskrit *smṛti* reminds us that the practice of *sati* helps us to recall our fundamental orientation to the precepts and path of the Buddha as we engage in observation of the self – thus implying that there is such a thing as *wrong* mindfulness: the mindfulness of, say, a terrorist preparing to detonate a bomb or attack civilians. The presence of *sampajāno* and *ātāpi* accompanying *sati* should preclude this.

This usage raises a question-mark over the appropriation of mindfulness as a practice of 'bare attention' by many contemporary users of the term.[6] In a perceptive essay, Robert Scharf notes that this notion of 'bare attention', as widely adopted today, has its origins in the teachings of the Burmese Master Mahāsī Sayādaw (1904–82), who stressed the development of *sati* at the expense of *samatha* and *jhāna* (Scharf 2015).[7] His student, Siegmund Feniger (1901–94), who took the name Nyanaponika Thera, popularized this notion of 'bare attention' in the West, especially through his 1954 book *The Heart of Buddhist Meditation* (Scharf 2015, p. 480, n. 6).[8] Although many contemporary Western practitioners of mindfulness preference the description of it as 'bare attention', following the arguments of Scharf and seeing it in context within the *Suttas* as concomitant with *sampajāna* and *ātāpi*, a strong case can be made that it is closer to the original Sanskrit 'remembrance' when evoked during contemplation. Following this line of argument, *sati* thus suggests a neutral observation of what is happening in the mind without cognitive intervention. Anālayo tells us that it requires 'uninvolved and detached receptivity' – silently observing 'without doing anything' (2003, p. 58) while Bhikkhu Bodhi describes it as 'lucid awareness of the phenomenal field' (2011, p. 22). It is, says Bodhi, 'a stance of *watchfulness* or *observation* towards one's own experience' (2011, p. 25).[9] With this before us, and remembering that *sati* in the *Satipaṭṭhāna Sutta* accompanies bodily sensations, feelings (*vedanā*), mind (*citta*) and mental/emotional qualities (*dhammas*), it could be argued, as some Buddhists have suggested to me, that 'heartfulness' would also be an equally acceptable English translation of the Pali *sati* rather than the more cognitive 'mindfulness'.[10] This would certainly accord with the argument presented in this book and in many ways 'heartfulness' is a better word for what we find in the Christian tradition rather than the more cognitive 'mindfulness'. That being so, with 'mindfulness' being the current buzz-word (like that other slippery term 'spirituality'), I shall continue to work with it for the remainder of the book but ask the reader to keep this caveat 'in mind'.

What follows ...

Consequently, the remainder of the book will have three objectives. First, as stated above, the need to initiate dialogue between the two traditions of Buddhism and Christianity. Second, to rediscover the tradition of mindfulness – or, better, heartfulness – that lies, I will argue, within the Christian tradition, and finally to present some practical exercises to enable readers to practise some of the techniques and examples presented here and hopefully integrate them into their lives. As I said earlier, it is of course not obligatory for you to follow these; however, I feel that the spirit and enjoyment of the book will be enhanced if you are able to engage with at least some of the exercises. It will certainly enhance your understanding of what people are referring to when they talk about mindfulness. The exercises I will recommend have arisen from my own encounters over three decades with some wise practitioners of meditation, and my hope is that they may be of use on your own spiritual journey as they have been to me. Consequently, I shall begin with the first:

Exercise One: The Gifts of Silence

The basis of prayer, mindfulness and contemplation is simplicity – I shall keep repeating this throughout the book. If you find any method or technique described here distracting or annoying, just move on to another one. This is not an examination or test with a diploma at the end! The exercises at the end of each chapter are basic stillness exercises to be used in tandem with the text. Meditation/mindfulness is really something that should be *done* rather than talked about.

'Be still and know'

It is difficult for human beings to be still. On a certain level we are not designed for it. We spend most of our waking hours following our instincts – searching for food, looking out for danger, listening to potential threats – that it is difficult for us to switch off. Stillness, meditation, prayer, mindfulness, contemplation – whatever name we give it – is possibly the simplest exercise for us and yet also paradoxically the most difficult. We are told what we need to do, but can we do it? Anthony de Mello SJ, the Indian Jesuit, talked of the need of developing a 'tolerance for silence' (De Mello 2010, p. 1) which – if pursued – will, he assures us, enable us to 'touch the wellsprings of life inside of us'. In his book on contemplative prayer, the American Trappist monk Thomas Merton, to whom we shall return later, quotes with approval Isaac of Nineveh, the Syrian monk (Merton 1973, pp. 33–4): 'if you love truth, be a lover of silence. Silence like the sunlight will illuminate you in God and will deliver you from the phantoms of ignorance.' He continues, 'in the beginning we have to force ourselves to be silent. But then there is born something that draws us to silence … If only you practise this, untold light will dawn on you in consequence … after a while a certain sweetness is born in the heart of this exercise and the body is drawn almost by force to remain in silence.'

So let us begin our series of exercises by trying to be silent together.

As with all exercises, whether physical, mental or spiritual, we need to take a little time to prepare ourselves. First, find a reasonably quiet spot where you will probably not get interrupted for 10–15 minutes or so. This of course is easier for some than others. Your prayer/meditation sessions may have to be dictated as to when there is less activity in your house or you can get away to somewhere quiet. Don't be too precious about the quiet aspect. Anthony de Mello always ran his prayer exercises near a busy road with the window open – quite a distraction in India! The reason being, he said, was because 'if you learn to take all the sounds that surround you into your contemplation you will discover that there is a deep silence in the heart of all sounds' (1984, p. 47). Thus to seek after perfect silence may be an unnecessary block to progress at the beginning of the prayer journey.

It is often wise to choose carefully the place you do these exercises. Some people insist on always occupying the same spot, perhaps surrounded by favourite and beloved items, holy pictures, etc. While routine can help, sometimes it pays to vary things and try other locations for these exercises – inside and outside the house, or a place of worship; in the open air, amid nature, etc. Try them on the train or bus on the way to work – you may be surprised how they transform the experience.

Once you have found a relatively secluded spot, now make yourself comfortable. Of course, posture is a large aspect of prayer and again many will have their own preferences. Whether you are sitting, kneeling, cross-legged or full lotus position, two golden rules apply: first, try to keep your back straight. This doesn't mean ram-rod straight (you are not on parade), but make sure the vertebrae are resting one upon the other, head resting level on the 'top of the pile'. If possible, imagine too a fine thread connecting the top of the head with the ceiling; this will help your posture. Second, try to be aware of your feet on the ground or bottom on the chair/earth. The prayer sessions will lead you into new places, so it is good to keep your feet firmly planted on the ground throughout.

So once you are in a comfortable position I ask you to be silent for ten minutes – set a timer or alarm if necessary.

That's it, just be still for ten minutes.

o O o

MINDFULNESS OR HEARTFULNESS?

Now, as mentioned earlier, this can be the easiest and the most demanding of exercises at the same time. We may panic, we may be overwhelmed by thoughts or feelings. We may feel physically uncomfortable and need to shift positions several times. At this stage all we have to do is observe the process. This exercise is the 'door to the castle' and it is important at this point just to observe the processes that are going on within and around us when we try to be silent.

First, as I say, there are the physical processes. We are physical beings who exist in the dimensions of this physical space. Somehow we shall have to work with that – which is something we shall return to in the next chapter.

Second, there are the whirring of our thoughts. The Buddhists have some good names for it. At one point it is compared to the monkey gathering fruit in the jungle – the famous 'monkey mind'. The Buddha goes so far at one point as to picture the mind as being like a wild crazy elephant – in rut! So, as with the body, we shall need to spend some time getting to know that crazy elephant.

Then there are our emotions. Always churning, never still, we can experience sadness, happiness, elation, depression or anger – all in the space of half an hour. It is what makes us human beings yet we are often terrified of these emotions. Carl Jung once said that we are 'pitifully ignorant of our selves – this is the most dangerous challenge of our times'.[11] As the Syrian monk Isaac of Nineveh said, silence will be the door to wisdom – even if we may not like some of the insights about ourselves that we will discover.

As well as bodily sensations, thoughts and feelings we shall imagine situations – past, present and future. We shall be aware of our prejudices, criticisms and other voices that we carry around with us. Finally, in all this there may also be that 'still, small voice' – the tiny 'sound of silence' that gives rest to the soul. But it may be hard to grasp!

o O o

So, a simple exercise but a vital one. If you can sit for ten minutes observing your efforts to be silent then you are halfway there – you have made the first step in one of the most important journeys of your life. For in all that turmoil and change, we have within us, as the Spanish saint Teresa of Avila described it, an 'interior castle' full of good things, fountains, labyrinths, great beauty and wisdom. It is our birthright and somehow we have locked ourselves out of that castle. What a tragedy! What a mystery! Stillness, silence and mindfulness will be the key that will enable us to unlock those creaky, rusty gates and re-enter our inheritance – reclaim what is rightfully ours.

Even if you found this exercise difficult, congratulate yourself. Just to see how difficult it is, is to have embarked upon the first step. You have glimpsed inside the castle even if at this stage you cannot get to the goal you seek. Don't worry, that will come. For at this stage just the simple act of awareness is sufficient to launch us off on our journey together.

Variations on the Exercise

Classic mindfulness programmes often start with the famous 'raisin exercise' developed by Jon Kabat-Zinn. In a way this is a variation of the above exercise but takes an object for attention – in this case, a simple raisin. We begin the process by observing the raisin, what St Ignatius of Loyola will call 'the application of the senses': we observe its size, colour, feel, smell, etc. Once we have acquainted ourselves with the raisin we pop it into our mouths and begin the slow process of masticating on it. We notice the sensations and tastes as the raisin slowly dissolves in our mouth. In contrast to the 'bare awareness' exercise with which I began, this one immediately brings in a strong sensual element. However, as before, the purpose will be to observe our feelings, reactions and thoughts, even if they are along the lines of 'What a strange exercise!', 'What am I doing this for?', 'Isn't it a bit daft?', etc. As with the sitting exercise, the secret is to keep an open, non-judgemental mind on the thoughts and feelings as they occur. Watch them, observe them and then let them pass. After all, it will all be over in ten minutes so you can resume your helter-skelter existence undeterred after this annoying break ...

This encounter with silence is what has often been referred to in the Christian tradition as the 'entry into the desert' – we shall explore the rich meaning and history of this encounter, and its lessons for our mindfulness practice today, in the next chapter.

Notes

1 London, January 2016.

2 Like 'mindfulness', the Pāli term *Dhamma* (Sanskrit: *Dharma*) is a central concept not only of Buddhism but of many South Asian religions. The term has connotations of a way of true being and living practised to lead to enlightenment.

3 In recent conversation and correspondence with the noted Buddhist scholar Rupert Gethin, he suggests that we have at least three phenomena going under the present label of 'mindfulness': first, clinical mindfulness as developed by practitioners such as Kabat-Zinn and Williams in their MBCT and MBSR courses. Second, mindfulness as a commercial phenomenon, promulgated by apps for making you a better worker, businessman, lover, etc. – what is sometimes called 'McMindfulness'. And finally, mindfulness as a new Western phenomenon that, in Gethin's words, 'eschews traditional Buddhist practices (such as devotional rituals) and the traditional framework of karma and rebirth, where the goal of nirvana is understood as liberation from the round of rebirth, and replaces these with a more therapeutic framework where nirvana is understood as a kind of equilibrium and state of well-being achieved by mindfulness meditation'. Such practitioners will still claim the title of being 'Buddhist' and hold that 'mindfulness' is, as they see it, the essence of Buddhism. At the time of writing it is still too early to say how these three strands might develop and interact.

4 'Right Mindfulness: The active, watchful mind'.

5 As Rupert Gethin points out (2011), Rhys Davids's translation was enormously influential on subsequent Buddhist studies and adopted by most scholars thereafter.

6 See, for example, Mace (2008) and Nyanaponika Thera (1994, p. 73): 'By bare attention we understand the clear and single-minded awareness of what actually happens to us and in us, at the successive moments of perception. It is called "bare" because it attends to the bare facts of perception without reacting to them by deed, speech or mental comment.'

7 *Samatha* and *Jhāna* are two aspects of the Buddhist path encountered by the practitioner. Again, difficult to translate, *Samatha* has connotations of 'clear abiding' as an insight into the true nature of mind, whereas the *Jhāna*s are higher contemplative states achieved through long practice; in the Western tradition they can be compared, for example, to the later mansions of St Teresa of Avila's *Interior Castle* to which we will return in a later chapter. For more on this analogy, see Cousins 1989.

8 Through his influence, among others, on teachers such as Jack Kornfield (b. 1945) and Joseph Goldstein (b. 1944).

9 As he puts it in a recent internet interview available on www.wisdompubs.org/author/bhikkhu-bodhi, mindfulness/*sati* is: 'A bending back of the stream of awareness upon one's own self, upon one's own immediate concrete experience – physical and mental – in order to bring clarity to that experience ... *Sati* is what keeps the object present before one's attention or, better, attentiveness.'

10 See, for example, the presentation at the American Academy of Religion in San Diego (2014) by Michael Spezio, Brent Field and Kevin Reimer: *Heartfulness as Mindfulness: Imitatio of Affectivity and Perspective in Christian Contemplative Practice*. The notion has been confirmed by conversations with Buddhist monks in India and Europe and is described in Ajahn Brahm's *Kindfulness* (2016).

11 Interview with John Freeman, *Face to Face*, BBC, 1959.

2

The Mindful Psychology of the Desert

Remain in your cell – it will teach you everything![1]

The metaphor and reality of the desert burns itself into the consciousness of at least three major world religions: Judaism, Christianity and Islam. All three arise from the desert and contain a *nostalgie* for former times when God first revealed God's self in the harsh burning environment of the wilderness. For the Jews it is the place where God revealed God's self to Moses at Horeb, appearing in the burning bush (Exodus 3), that very essence of the dry, desiccated wasteland within which Moses found himself at that time. It was the inhospitable place within which the people of Israel were tested for 40 years as God played cat and mouse with their hopes, expectations and theological understandings, culminating in the revelations of God's nature and covenant on the inhospitable peak of Sinai (Exodus 19). After the deportation and exile to Babylon the prophets looked back nostalgically to their people's time in the desert and longed once again for God to lure and 'seduce them' (Hosea 2.14) back to the wilderness where the Valley of Suffering would once again become the 'door of hope'. There, they sang, Israel 'shall respond as in the days of her youth, as at the time when she came out of the land of Egypt' (Hosea 2).

Likewise, Christianity 'appears in the wilderness' in the shape of the quasi-shamanic figure of St John the Baptist. He emerges from the desert, writes St Mark, 'clothed with camel's hair, with a leather belt around his waist' eating 'locusts and wild honey' (Mark 1). This child of the desert, a true prophetic soul, wild and unkempt, pulled no punches in his dealings with the powers and authorities of the city – the classic antithesis to the desert dwellers – sharing with his master, Jesus, a delight in challenging those in power.

John arises from the desert and Jesus, we are told in Matthew 4, begins his ministry there – his first act after his baptism at the hands of John. Thus, at the start of his ministry Jesus withdraws immediately to the desert to begin battle with the devil – that traditional inhabitant of the wasteplaces. We shall have more to say about him and his little demon helpers later.

Thus from its earliest beginnings Christianity recognizes the importance of entry into the desert as a *necessary stage* in the spiritual journey. Its importance in the earliest stages of Christianity (for example, St Paul after his conversion spends time in the deserts of Arabia described in Galatians 1) means that it becomes 'archetypal' for all Christian spirituality that will follow. Of course, as Christianity unfolds this will not necessarily be about actually entering the physical desert of the Middle East. For the early Celtic Christians at the western fringes of Europe, their desert was to be found in the wild and untameable ocean besides which they would often live or upon which they would set out on voyages of spiritual self-discovery. As the late Middle Ages collapsed into the modern age and the growth of the cities reduced the terrain of the desert, the new orders such as the Carmelites stressed the importance of finding the desert in the city. St Teresa of Avila, in her reform of the order in the sixteenth century, insisted that her 'carmels', her 'little deserts', should be placed at the centre and heart of the cities of sixteenth-century Spain where, by and large, they remain to this day. In the twentieth century the Italian Little Brother of Jesus Carlo Carretto felt that the desert was to be found in the city and made sure that the order he founded, the Little Brothers and Sisters of Jesus, would live in the most rundown, socially deprived inner-city estates. Today the sisters and brothers in the UK live in the hardest hit neighbourhoods of huge cities such as Birmingham and London.

So, as Christianity emerged, 'desert spirituality', as it is often called, emerged too. Not just a physical dwelling in the desiccated or abandoned places, but also a dwelling in the inhospitable places within. An invitation to all people to move out of their comfort zones and move to the places of loss, driven-ness, pain and grief that our ordinary lives so deftly and easily mask through addictions, consumerisms, promiscuities, greeds and violence. For us twenty-first-century children of Freud and Jung it is the place of the unconscious where we are no longer in control and more primitive and basic urges and desires take over. It is, ultimately, a spirituality of paradox for, we are told, it is in the uncomfortable places that we do most to avoid that God chooses to reveal God's self to us. Here we will find the 'living water' that ultimately we are seeking – not in forests, cities and verdant places, but in the neglected, dry and dead places on our earth and in our selves: the same place we encountered in our first exercise at the end of Chapter 1.

Who were the desert fathers and mothers?

In the Christian tradition our eternal guides to this strange half-world of suppressed desire and refashioned self are the group of Christians who went to live in the deserts of the Middle East around the time that Christianity became a 'state-sponsored religion' after the conversion of the Roman Emperor Constantine to Christianity in AD 312. Around this time we first read reports of large numbers of Christians, perhaps disaffected with the newfound alliance between crown and Church, making their way towards the deserts of Egypt, Gaza and Syria. By AD 324 we find the first reference to a *monachos* (literally, 'a solitary one' from whence we derive our English word 'monk') as a witness in a lawsuit (see Dunn 2003, p. 1).

Traditionally, the movement begins on a Sunday morning around AD 270/271 when a young Egyptian Christian, known as Anthony, goes to church and hears the Gospel reading from

Matthew 19.21: 'If you wish to be perfect, go, sell your possessions, and give the money to the poor, and you will have treasure in heaven; then come, follow me.'

Unlike many Christians – before and since – who hear these words and do nothing about them, Anthony, so we are told in his biography later written by St Athanasius, took these words to heart, sold all his possessions, and went out into the desert to pursue the life of a wandering ascetic (see White 1998). From Anthony onwards, it seems that an oral tradition develops in the wasteplaces of Egypt, Syria and Palestine which finally begins to be written down in the Semitic languages of the Middle East before being recorded and written down in Greek as the *Apophthegmata* or *Sayings of the Desert Fathers and Mothers*. These have recently received excellent translations into English by Sr Benedicta Ward of Oxford and it is on her translations that I rely.

What do the monks do?

After many years in the desert Anthony was approached by a group of people asking, 'What do the monks do?' His reply: the monk is the one who fights demons. This is such a fundamental statement regarding the nature of desert spirituality that it is worth reflecting upon it a little more. If we think of demons or devils at all today we are probably going to visualize pantomime or Hallowe'en creatures with painted red horns and a pointed tail. When the desert fathers and mothers use the term it is far more subtle and perhaps nearer to what we would today call a 'psychological' understanding of the self.

A good example of this is found in the writing of Evagrius Ponticus in the *Praktikos* and the *Chapters on Prayer* where he uses the Greek term *logismoi* interchangeably with *daimones* for what we would call 'demons' and 'passions'.[2] Following in the tradition of Anthony and identifying the influences of the evil one with our own passions and movements of the soul, Evagrius is able to produce an anthropology that is both provocative and authentic.

Like Gregory Nazianzen (*Praktikos* 89), Evagrius divides the person into three elements. First is a 'concupiscible element' (*epithumia*) that is attracted to facets of the world primarily through the bodily desires of food, sex and wealth. It is the element of the soul that seeks comfort and pleasure. Not so far away from Freud's 'pleasure principle', in the Middle Ages it would transmogrify into the three 'deadly sins' of lust, greed and jealousy. The second element is the so-called 'irascible element' (*thumos*) that is the part of the soul that separates us from the world around us through violence and anger. In Freudian terms it is close to his notion of the 'death instinct' or *thanatos* and would become the three deadly sins of anger, sloth and envy. Over and above these two elements is the 'rational' part of the soul, the *logistikon*, which like Plato's charioteer in the *Phaedrus* (246–54) directs the other two parts of the soul. However, as the other passions can be directed against God, so too this aspect of the soul can be directed against God through the overarching sin of pride.

When we think of these passions in a Christian context we often see them as negative aspects of the self. Within the desert tradition these passions are essentially *neutral* in themselves. This cannot be over-emphasized. So many Christians are weighed down with the dualist assumption that the passions are bad in themselves. Nothing could be further from the message of the desert fathers and mothers. As Isaiah of Scetis states in his *Ascetical Discourses*, all the passions are sacred in themselves, it is just that we have redirected them by our wills so that they become turned against God (Chryssavgis 2003, p. 61). Anger, as used by Christ in the temple, can be directed to good and holy things – in psychological terms, it creates our space in the world and upholds personal dignity and worth. Regarding sexual desire I doubt if most of us would be here without it: sexual desire is part of the mechanics of the universe that allows affectivity and warmth into our relations with others. It is when anger and sexual desire, for example, become twisted or perverted towards gratifying individual egotistical needs at the expense of others that problems emerge. So, within the desert tradition we have a continued emphasis on the need to redirect and transform these passions rather than destroy them. In Freudian terms, there is the danger of control through repression and suppression which is ultimately fruitless for the suppressed desire will control us even more than when it was unsuppressed!

Even more remarkable are the passages in the fathers and mothers where we hear that 'everything that goes to excess comes from the demons' (Abba Poemen 31). That is, not just the passions but even Christian pieties and practices such as fasting, prayer and vigils may become in themselves loveless and egotistical acts. St Anthony recalls 'demons singing the psalms while remaining invisible, shocking as it is to tell. In addition they recite the sacred words of Scripture with a foul mouth ... they also awaken to prayer those who are asleep, so as to deprive them of sleep for the whole night' (*The Life of St Anthony* 25, in White 1998). One of the key elements of *diakresis* or 'the discernment of spirits' so central to the Christian spiritual tradition, and to which we will return later, is that an apparently good action, deed or thought may have a harmful purpose or end. Time and again the desert fathers and mothers exhort their followers to follow the advice of St Paul and to 'examine yourselves and test yourselves' (2 Corinthians 13.5; see *The Life of St Anthony* 55); this 'self knowledge' will be a recurring theme in the Christian tradition of spirituality.

Thus, we find in the desert fathers and mothers a moral anthropology that exhorts us to redirect the passions from the destructive and towards the constructive – but always remembering the advice of the elders that this must not take place in too hard or harsh an environment that breaks the individual through excessive penances. As St Anthony explains in a famous passage:

A hunter in the desert saw Abba Anthony enjoying himself with the brethren and was shocked. Wanting to show him that it was necessary sometimes to meet the needs of the brethren, the old man said to him, 'Put an arrow in your bow and shoot it'. So he did. The old man then said, 'Shoot another', and he did so. Then the old man said, 'Shoot yet again', and the hunter replied 'If I bend my bow so much I will break it'. Then the old man said to him, 'It is the same with the work of God. If we stretch the brethren beyond measure they will soon break.' (*Sayings* 13)

John Cassian, another important chronicler of the sayings and works of the desert elders, quotes with approval in his *Conferences* (2.16.1) an old Greek saying: 'extremes meet' and continues 'for the extreme of fasting comes to the same end as overeating does, and excessive prolongation of a vigil is as detrimental to a monk as the torpor of heavy sleep is'. The fathers and mothers wisely counsel that we must always examine our *motives* for everything we do, not least our pious and penitential acts. These, as we have seen, are not above the action of the destructive and harmful forces within ourselves. The aim of the desert fathers and mothers is not therefore to seek penance for penance's sake, but to engage in *ascesis* or 'training' to enable us to come closer to God. For them, there is a clear distinction between this 'training' of desire and suppression or repression of desire.

As the desert teachings later found their way into Western monasticism through the writings of John Cassian, this spirit of moderation and balance would be preserved and enshrined in Benedict's famous *Rule for Beginners*, the foundation of Western monasticism.

Mindful silence: fighting the demons

We have then identified the key trope of 'desert' as holding the central Christian message that God is to be found in the wasteplaces and dead spaces of the heart. In this poisonous wilderness, as Carl Jung would later say in the twentieth century, we can find gold. The aim of the process, as we have seen, is the redirection of the essentially neutral passions back towards God.

How then can this be done? What counsel do the fathers and mothers give us to attempt this? Apart from the importance of balance which we have already mentioned we can highlight two key concerns: stability and silence, both of which will be key elements of what we could term a 'desert psychology of mindfulness'. Stability, 'staying with', lies at the heart of the desert approach to dealing with the *logismoi*. This will later be enshrined in the *Rule of St Benedict* as the vow of stability that all Western monks must make. What is meant by this?

The essential notion is that when confronted with a passion in our spiritual search, whether that is anger, lust, fear or greed, we should 'stay with' the passion in prayer. With time, the elders advise us, we shall see it transform into another passion or, in many cases, disappear altogether. As Abba Poemen puts it: 'If someone shuts a snake and a scorpion up in a bottle, in time they will be completely destroyed. So it is with evil thoughts: they are suggested by the demons; they disappear through patience' (*Sayings* 1).

Benedict and his disciples were suspicious of the spiritual tourist, a phenomenon sadly all too common in our own times – the seeker who moves from place to place, seeking perhaps a spiritual high but not staying long enough to get to the roots of their restlessness. As one of the mothers, Amma Syncletica, wrote: 'If you find yourself in a monastery do not go to another place, for that will harm you a great deal. Just as the bird who abandons the eggs she was sitting on prevents them from hatching, so the monk or the nun grows cold and their faith dies when they go from one place to another' (*Sayings* 6).

This counsel of patience goes to the heart of the work of the desert and with it an indifference to charismata, gifts of the spirit and extraordinary spiritual highs and experiences that sometimes accompany prolonged spiritual reflection. The elders remind us that Christianity is not a religion that devotes itself to pursuing spiritual highs, but that all Christian spirituality is to be measured by the effects it has on the world and our being in that world (see *The Life of St Anthony* 38, in White 1998). In this vein it is worth noting that as well as the seven passions we outlined above, the fathers and mothers had an eighth vice they had to struggle with – what they called *accidie* or *acedia*, and which does not really translate into English, though 'listlessness or restlessness' might do. Evagrius' description of it is so finely drawn and wise that it is worth quoting in full:

> The demon of *acedia* – also called the noonday demon – is the one that causes the most serious trouble of all. He presses his attack upon the monk about the fourth hour (around 10 am) and besieges the soul until the eighth hour (around 2 pm). First of all he makes it seem that the sun barely moves, if at all, and that the day is fifty hours long. Then he constrains the monk to look constantly out the windows, to walk outside the cell, to gaze carefully at the sun to determine how far it stands from the ninth hour (lunchtime), to look now this way and now that to see if one of the brothers might ... might ...
>
> Then too he instills in the heart of the monk a hatred for the place, a hatred for his very life itself, a hatred for manual labor ...
>
> Should there be someone at this period who happens to offend him in some way or other, this too the demon uses to contribute further to his hatred. This demon drives him along to desire other sites where he can more easily procure life's necessities, more readily find work and make a real success of himself. He goes on to suggest that, after all, it is not the place that is the basis of pleasing the Lord, God is to be adored

everywhere. He joins to these reflections the memory of his dear ones and of his former way of life.

He depicts life stretching out for a long period of time, and brings before the mind's eye the toil of the ascetic struggle and, as the saying has it, leaves no leaf unturned to induce the monk to forsake his cell and drop out of the fight. (*Praktikos* 12)

The passage is classic Evagrius: psychologically subtle and with not a little humour as he holds up the mirror to the wannabe student of spiritual struggle, showing how easily one is swerved from 'staying with' the difficulties and hardships of the spiritual life, often in the name of 'making a real success of himself'. Yet, as Evagrius makes clear, 'no other demon follows close upon the heels of this one (when he is defeated) but only a state of deep peace and inexpressible joy arise out of this struggle'. Rather than being a curse, *accidie* can be the gateway to a deep peace for the individual. If the seeker can 'stay with' all the distractions and boredoms of the cell, then great peace will be found.

As we have seen, when we embark on the path of mindful contemplation we will inevitably encounter these inner demons of restlessness. The fathers and mothers give us the good counsel to just 'stay with them'. They assure us that slowly, as we observe their vagaries, the eternal silence of the soul will be restored.

Accordingly, the second key tool in the seeker's fight with the passions is silence or *hesychia*. This is not so much a physical silence as a silence of the heart. As Abba Poemen puts it: 'A man may seem to be silent, but if his heart is condemning others he is babbling ceaselessly. But there may be another who talks from morning till night and yet he is truly silent; that is, he says nothing that is not profitable' (*Sayings* 27). This silence or *contemplatio* lies at the heart of the Christian contemplative tradition and is most difficult to describe. James Finley, the contemporary writer and disciple of Thomas Merton whom we shall meet later, called it a 'subtle nothingness', and the English Dominican Herbert McCabe lovingly called it 'a waste of time with God'. John Chryssavgis in his *Heart of the Desert* describes it as:

> A way of waiting, a way of watching and a way of listening ... it is a way of interiority, of stopping and then of exploring the cellars of the heart and the centre of life ... Silence is never merely a cessation of words ... rather it is the pause that holds together all the words both spoken and unspoken. Silence is the glue that connects our attitudes and actions. It is fullness not emptiness, it is not an absence but the awareness of a presence. (Chryssavgis 2003, pp. 45–6)

John Cassian in his *Conferences* refers to this quality of the seeker as *purity of heart* and sees it as one of the key elements in the spiritual search revealed in the perpetual practice of prayer. This is not just about specific bounded 'prayer periods' but it pertains rather to a whole *attitude* and disposition of the person, a distinction perhaps between 'prayer' and 'prayerfulness'. As Cassian states in Conference Nine:

> Whatever our soul was thinking about before the time of prayer inevitably occurs to us when we pray as a result of the operation of the memory. Hence what we would like to be during the time of prayer we should strive to be outside of prayer. For the mind in prayer is shaped by the state that it was previously in, and, when we sink into prayer, the image of the same deeds, words and thoughts plays itself out before our eyes. This makes us angry or sad, depending upon our previous condition, or it recalls past lusts or business. (*Conferences* 9.3.3)

In modern computer jargon – 'Garbage In, Garbage Out!' The disposition of the person before prayer affects the nature of their prayer and the aim of the pray-er is to purify thoughts and actions so that, in Cassian's rather poetic description, the 'light feather or plume' of the soul can have its impurities, mud and dampness removed so that it may be 'naturally borne to the heavenly heights by the slightest breath' (*Conferences* 9.4.1). We shall see later this influence continuing throughout the Christian tradition up to the present day.

Mindfulness and the desert tradition

Having looked at Buddhist and contemporary notions of mindfulness in the previous chapter, I would like to conclude this chapter by looking more closely at the writings of the desert elders, especially those of Evagrius and Cassian, in order to see what they can tell us about the contemporary engagement with mindfulness from a Christian perspective. Before we do this, however, it is worth reminding ourselves of the two aspects of the Christian contemplative tradition that we highlighted earlier in comparison with the programme of mindfulness in the contemporary world. First, as I stated above, I think the Christian prayer tradition is best understood as a dialogue of head and heart – it is not simply cognitive as some of the contemporary strands of mindfulness suggest. In this respect, the Christian prayer tradition can be contrasted with some of the notions of 'bare attention' that we encountered earlier. The Christian way of mindfulness is a Prayer of the Heart. It is as much heartfulness as mindfulness.

Second, in contrast to some of the Buddhist and psychological models we explored earlier, the Christian path is one that clearly acknowledges the transcendental/transpersonal within the human personality (see Tyler 2016). Christian prayer/mindfulness can be distinguished from Buddhist prayer in that for the Christian there is always a transcendental perspective on the soul. This may be the case in some of the types of Buddhist prayer we explored earlier, but it is not necessarily so. With these two caveats in mind, then, we can turn our attention to the writings of the desert fathers on prayer.

One of the classic formulations of prayer from the desert tradition comes from Evagrius of Pontus' treatise *On Prayer*, where he states that: 'Prayer is a conversation of the spirit with God. Seek therefore the disposition that the spirit needs, in order to be able to reach out towards its Lord and to hold converse with him without any intermediary' (*On Prayer* 3, in Clément 2013, p. 181). What is immediately striking in this definition is that the two distinguishing aspects of Christian prayer highlighted are evident – that prayer/meditation is a relationship with the Transcendent One and, second, that it is a loving relationship based on devotion and adoration. Further, Evagrius outlines the third key element of the Christian notion of contemplation – that it is a conversation 'without any intermediary'. Such a conversation takes place in the intimacy of our hearts with Christ. Where and when is a question for the individual seeker for, as Francisco de Osuna stated many years later in his treatise on prayer, *The Third Spiritual Alphabet*, there are a thousand types of people and a thousand types of prayer (Osuna 6.1 – we shall return to Osuna in a later chapter; see also Cassian's *Conferences* 9.8). Clément, in his masterly exposition of prayer in the early Christian tradition, points out that posture and position, as practised in the East, were not so important to the early Christians. He quotes, for example, Origen's text 'On Prayer':

> Certainly there are countless attitudes of the body, but that in which we stretch out our hands and lift our eyes to heaven is to be preferred for expressing with the body the dispositions of the soul during prayer ... But circumstances may lead us to pray sitting down, for example when we have a pain in the legs, or even in bed because of fever. For the same reason, if for example we are on board ship or if our business does not allow us to withdraw to perform our duty in regard to prayer, it is possible to pray without taking up any particular outward attitude. ... As for the place, you should realise that every place is suitable for prayer ... However in order to pray

undisturbed it is possible to choose a particular place in one's house, if practicable, as a kind of hallowed spot, and to pray there. (*On Prayer* 31)

As to establishing what happens in this 'Christian mindfulness' as promoted by these early fathers, I would like to concentrate on the passages in Cassian's *Conferences* where he discusses prayer, in particular *Conferences* Nine and Ten. Key to Cassian's notion of prayer is the establishment of what he sometimes calls 'purity of heart' and at other times 'tranquillity':

> And when the mind (*mens*) has been established in tranquillity (*in tranquillitate*) and has been freed from the bonds of every fleshly passion (*omnium passionum carnalium*), and the heart's attention is unwaveringly fastened upon the one and highest good, it will fulfil the apostolic words: 'Pray without ceasing.' (1 Thessalonians 5.17)[3]

For:

> When the thoughts of the mind have been seized by this purity (*in hac puritate*) and have been refashioned from earthly dullness to the likeness of the spiritual and the angelic, whatever they take in, whatever they reflect upon, and whatever they do will be most pure and sincere prayer.[4] (*Conferences* 9.7)

Here we see Cassian adopting a familiar trope of the early desert fathers and mothers (and one familiar to our Buddhist friends) – that the self is at war with itself. We have anxieties, disturbances and sufferings that we need to resolve through the practice of prayer as we try to develop his 'tranquillity of mind':

> When our mind finds further occasions for spiritual thoughts, others creep back in and those that had been laid hold of slip rapidly away. Thus our soul (*animus*) has no constancy of its own, nor does it possess of its own power any immutability

with regard to holy thoughts even when it seems somehow or other to hold on to them.[5]

Like Evagrius (and ultimately Plato – see Tyler 2016), there is no constancy to the mind. Again, this is close to the Buddhist psychology we looked at earlier. For Cassian, then, the purpose of prayer/meditation is to produce that *stabilitas cordis* or *puritatis mentis* where the wandering mind will be held in stability: 'According to the degree of purity to which each mind has attained and according to the nature of the condition either to which it has declined because of what happened to it or to which it has renewed itself by its own efforts, these change at every moment.'[6]

Much of this resembles some of the Buddhist notions of mindfulness we outlined in the previous chapter; however, what is striking in the Christian tradition of mindfulness is that the notion of 'bare attention' needs to be linked with loving devotion to the Saviour. In this respect, Cassian follows the example of the other early fathers in adding to his neo-Platonic conception of the soul the sense of devotion that we find in the Christian Scriptures. Here, for example, he quotes St Paul's first letter to Timothy: 'I urge that supplications, prayers, intercessions, and thanksgivings should be made for everyone' (1 Timothy 2.1). From this idea Cassian goes on to expound his notion of four types of prayer available to the Christian seeker (9.9 onwards): *supplication*, *prayer*, *intercession* and *thanksgiving*. He defines the four modes thus:

1 *Supplication* (*obsecratio*) is 'an imploring or a petition concerning sins, by which a person who has been struck by compunction begs for pardon for their present or past misdeeds' (*Conferences* 9.11).
2 *Prayers* (*oratio*) are 'those acts by which we offer or vow something to God' (*Conferences* 9.12). This, according to Cassian, is an attitude whereby we place ourselves in right relationship with the transcendent.

3 *Intercessions* (*postulatio*) are those prayers 'we are accustomed to make for others when our spirits are fervent, beseeching on behalf of our dear ones and for the peace of the whole world' (*Conferences* 9.13). This we could call the horizontal aspect of Christian prayer whereby we remember those around us and relate to them. We shall return to this later in the book.
4 Finally, *thanksgiving* (*gratia*) is the means whereby 'recalling God's past benefits contemplating his present ones or foreseeing what great things God has prepared for those who love him, offered to the Lord in unspeakable ecstasies (*per excessus ineffabiles*)' (*Conferences* 9.14). Again we shall return to this sense of Christian prayer throughout the book.

Mindfulness in this early Christian sense, then, cannot be divorced from its place in the early Christian schema of devotion to the Transcendent Other coupled with the need for dedicated action to our fellow human beings (just as the early Buddhist sense of mindfulness is connected with the need for dissolution of the bonds of *dukkha* by contemplation of non-self).[7] We shall return to all four elements, as defined by Cassian, throughout the book as they form a crucial basis for the understanding of Christian mindfulness as we will develop it here.

All four stages of prayer, for Cassian, are preparations or stages for the final ecstatic bliss of wordless union intimated in the final category of thanksgiving – that is, the 'exceedingly fervent and fiery prayers' (*preces ferventissimas et ignitas*) as the lover is united with the Divine Beloved (*Conferences* 9.15.1). For Cassian, this is experienced especially by those who attain the purity of mind and stability of heart (*stabilitas cordis*) – producing 'fiery prayer which can be neither seized nor expressed by the mouth of humans'. Again, this is another theme emerging through the future history of Christian prayer and one that we shall return to later.

Cassian finishes his exposition by relating these four types of prayer first to the example of Christ and his Passion and through the schema of the petitions of the Lord's Prayer, which for Cassian perfectly demonstrate his five levels of prayer/meditation. This is a theme we shall see taken up later by, among others, Teresa of Avila.

In summary, then, what we find in Cassian is a view of Christian prayer that follows the Trinitarian model of Christ praying to the Father as the basis or template for all future Christian meditation (as we stated at the outset of this book). Simply put, he describes Christian prayer as having two axes: a vertical, transcendental-immanent axis whereby the lover seeks the Beloved, and a horizontal-communal axis whereby all true Christian prayer will lead to action in the world, especially manifest in alleviating the suffering of one's fellow human beings. Prayer/mindfulness, then, in this early Christian sense, is not a means to an end but an end in itself – and one could say it is what makes us human. We are who we are by virtue of this essential aspect of our being. As he states: 'In it [his concept of prayer] there is contained no request for riches, no allusion to honours, no demand for power and strength, no mention of bodily health or of temporal existence' (*Conferences* 9.24).

In this respect, the current fashion of finding mindfulness helpful to alleviate physical symptoms in oneself would not be part of Cassian's understanding of the practice. The need for prayer, as with so many of the desert elders, is for Cassian a fundamental part of what it is to be a human being. Finally, it is worth stating that the aim of the encounter is not just a conversation, but for the lover to *be transformed* into the Lover. This, technically, we term 'deification'. Isaac of Nineveh described it thus: 'When the Spirit dwells in a person, from the moment in which that person has become prayer, he never leaves him. For the Spirit himself never ceases to pray in him. Whether the person is asleep or awake, prayer never from then on departs from his soul ... Prayer never again deserts him' (*Ascetic Treatises* 85, in Clément 2013, p. 210).

The path of Christian mindfulness, according to the desert elders, can thus be summarized as a practice that leads to awareness of the transcendent in the immanent through transformation of self in communion with the transcendent Beloved. Such prayer will, by necessity, be bound to an essential horizontal axis of action in the world.

Lessons for today

Each year I introduce my students to the marvellous literature of the desert tradition and each year they are impressed by the deep wisdom of these wise teachers. However, as we harvest the wisdom of the desert for today's world we have to realize that the luxury of leaving all and setting off alone into the desert is not one that most of us can afford. If we were to do it, it is doubtful that even there, in Sinai and Gaza, we would be able to avoid satellite TV or the mobile phone. Rather, contemporary spiritual commentators have tried to distil the essence of desert wisdom, much as I have done in this chapter, and see how we can turn to the 'desert within'. For, as has been stressed throughout this chapter, the physical desert – with its thorns, cacti and venomous reptiles – can be seen as a cipher or symbol for the desiccated deserts that we all carry within and which we will inevitably encounter whenever we engage in any mindfulness or contemplative practice. These are the inner psychological deserts so familiar to the alcoholic, the workaholic, the over-indulgent, the proud and the cantankerous. If we embark on a programme of prayer or mindfulness it won't be long, I can assure you, before we enter our own inner unpleasant deserts. Accordingly, I have suggested in this chapter that we can find a fruitful cross-over between the wisdom of the desert and contemporary perspectives of mindfulness and psychology. As we have seen, the desert fathers and mothers offer a wise, gentle and considerate Christian perspective on the art of tackling these seemingly inextirpable desires by the simple remedies and medication of discernment, prayer, balance and compassion. As the success of TV shows such as *The*

Monastery and *The Great Silence* demonstrate, these simple monastic remedies can still offer the seeker so much today (see Jamison 2006). As we outline the nature and role of the relationship between mindfulness and Christian prayer in the rest of this book, we shall find ourselves time and again returning to our spiritual 'granddaddies and mummies' – the desert fathers and mothers – who were truly the first practitioners of Christian mindfulness or, better, heartfulness.

Exercise Two: Body Scan

'We are human beings, not angels', wrote Teresa of Avila, therefore we need to take our bodies seriously. Body awareness is the bread and butter of prayer/meditation and every session should always include some form of it, no matter how cursory. Yet many of us live, as James Joyce once said, a little removed from our bodies. Trauma, embarrassment or just simple busyness keep us alienated from our bodily home, 'the temple of the Holy Spirit' as St Paul famously described it.

As before, we make the usual preparations – routine will be a good friend on our journey. So, we find a reasonably quiet spot where we will probably not get interrupted, and make ourselves comfortable. We remember our two golden rules: back straight but not ram-rod straight and feet on the floor/bottom on the chair/floor – what my friend Chris Cullen calls FOFBOC. Once in position we can begin – with the ground. Feel the ground beneath your feet and under your bottom. Notice it holding you up, gently and strongly, and slowly become aware of the sensations in your feet: tingling, numbness, pressure. The feel of the sock or shoe, tightness of cloth, differences of temperature.

As we pass through what is called the 'body scan', just be aware of the bodily sensations. Don't comment upon them, just notice them and pass on. If it helps, imagine a small torch moving slowly up the body, picking up and highlighting certain areas before moving on. Again, if it helps, close your eyes. Some prefer to keep their eyes open, others half closed – find what suits you best. As we become aware of the body we may need to shift position slightly – don't be worried about doing this.

Now turn the attention to the legs. As before, pass along and notice the sensations – tightness, cloth, heat, coolness, pressure, tension, relaxation. If you notice an area where you cannot feel anything, just spend a few moments at that spot to see if any sensations start to show themselves.

Now turn your attention to your hands. Notice the thousands of sensations there, along the fingers, the tip of the fingers, the thumbs, nails. Notice again feelings of warmth and coolness, moisture or dryness, tension or relaxation, before moving your attention gently up the arms until you reach the shoulders. If you find tensions along the way, just shake yourself gently to release them. As I said before, you don't need to be ram-rod straight – you are not on parade!

Now turn your attention to the belly, internal organs and heart. Notice the gentle rising and falling of the chest as the breath comes in and out. Don't try to alter the rhythm of the breath, just notice it. We shall return to the breath in the next exercise, but for now just note the presence of your friendly companion, always there, always reliable.

Now move to the neck and throat areas. Pay attention to the breath in the nostrils, and notice the cool air entering the nose and mouth and the warm air leaving. Inside the mouth notice the thousands of sensations around the teeth and tongue.

Move slowly now to the rest of the face, the eyes, ears and forehead. Finally, end with the very top of your head, trying if possible to be aware of it.

When you are ready, open your eyes and gently move your body again.

o O o

Hopefully, this most gentle of exercises will have helped you get in touch with your body in the here and now. It may be a pleasant experience (some people fall asleep when they do this – don't worry about it, it just means you are tired and need some rest). On the other hand, it may be an unpleasant experience, and you may encounter some aches or pains that you hadn't previously been aware of. If this is the case, it is important to remember that the exercises don't create pain (or shouldn't), but rather you have simply *become aware* of a pain that was probably there all the time but you had not been conscious of it. I have practised this exercise twice a day for the past 30 years and have done it with innumerable groups over that time. Generally speaking, people find it entirely relaxing and positive. In the cases where it isn't, there may be either a problem with your posture – try a different chair or cushion – or something physically wrong, in which case make an appointment with your doctor. Later on we shall work on the thoughts and feelings that arise during this type of 'body scan'. For now, just concentrate on the body sensations and try not to pay too much attention to the thoughts – as I say, we shall return to these later. Many of us, sadly, live too much in our heads. This simple exercise takes us from our heads into our bodies – often an unfamiliar place for many of us, but territory we need to get to know none the less.

Variations on the Exercise

After trying the above a few times you may want to spend a meditation session just concentrating on one area of the body – it may be the tip of the nose, forehead, cheek or lips. As you stay with the small area, just notice the sensations as they arise but try to resist the urge to scratch or interfere. Just let the sensations arise, flower and die away again. This is a deceptively simple exercise but meditators with many years of practice may still have trouble with this one. It can require a lot of concentration. However, if this 'one-pointed' concentration can be acquired it can prove extremely helpful later on.

If it is difficult to control thoughts during this exercise, then take a few words from the Scriptures or the sayings of the saints to recite as you practise the exercise:

>'Be still and know that I am God.'
>'O Lord, you know me completely.'
>'It was you who formed my inmost parts.'
>'I am fearfully and wonderfully made.'
>'You hold me in the palm of your hand.'
>'Always walking together – the body and the spirit.'
>'We are not angels, we have bodies.'

Notes

1 Saying of Abba Moses – *Sayings of the Desert Fathers*, in Ward 1984.

2 Thus the three movements of the soul – lust, *accidie* and pride – are called 'daimones' by Evagrius; gluttony, sadness and vainglory are called *logismoi*, and anger and avarice are 'passions'/'*pathos*'. For a deeper exploration of this text, see Tyler 2016.

3 'Porro quum mens fundata fuerit in tranquillitate praefata atque a nexibus omnium passionum carnalium absoluta, et illi uni ac summo bono adhaeserit tenacissima intentione, implebit apostolicum illud: Sine intermissione orate.'

4 'Nempe sensu mentis absorpto in hac puritate, et eodem reformato de situ terreno ad similitudinem spiritualem atque angelicam, quidquid in se receperit, egerit, sive tractaverit, erit oratio quaedam purissima.'

5 'Quumque mens nostra repererit alias quaslibet spiritualium sensuum occasiones, rursus aliis apprehensionibus irruentibus, spirituales meditations quae apprehensae fuerunt, lubrica volubilitate diffugiunt: ita ut animus noster nullam sui constantiam retinens, nec potestate propria possidens stabilitatem cogitationum sanctarum, videatur eas fortuitu, et non ex proposito seu industria concepisse, etiam tunc quam eas aliqualiter retinet.'

6 Nam et ipsa mens momentis singulis reformatur secundum mensuram puritatis qua proficit, et juxta qualitatem status in quem ex supervenientibus inclinator, vel per suam renovator industriam.' This quote has shades of the Origenist heresy that saw people as having fallen souls akin to some of the ideas in Plato. For more on the history of this and its implications for Christian spiritual anthropology, see Tyler 2016.

7 *Dukkha* is another key term in Buddhist thought and again difficult to translate. Put simply, it is the sense of suffering and alienation we experience living in this existence.

3

The Iberian School of Mindfulness and Mental Prayer

Tea-time at Montserrat

Tea-time at Montserrat.
The mountain slowly awakes from her siesta.
The Holy Bells
Begin their summons.
Birds,
Tired tourists,
Silvery Barcelona beyond,
God,
The world:
The Madonna's tears embrace us all.[1]

The Spanish 'Golden Age'

As the medieval period waned and the Iberian peninsula entered the modern era certain conditions came together to produce a flowering of contemplative writing in Iberia's 'Golden Age'. In his monumental study of this Spanish mystical writing between 1500 and 1700, the Spanish author Melquíades Andrés Martín stresses the continuity within the Spanish mystical tradition and its origins in the reform movements at the end of the fifteenth century (Andrés Martín 1975). These movements were often contradictory and unclear and he notes:

> This reform movement oscillated between the study of theology, revivified by the Dominicans, and a certain anti-intellectualism, which would initially invoke a certain anti-verbosity, within the Franciscans and Augustinians, and much later affective prayer (*oración afectiva*) which placed

more value on experience and love over study and intellect. (Andrés Martín 1975, p. 2)[2]

With reference to a favoured expression for prayer used by these authors, Andrés Martín refers to these authors as *'los recogidos'* – literally 'the recollected ones'. The use of the term *recogimiento* is instructive as it reminds us of the memory or recalling functions of *sati* discussed in Chapter 1. For the Iberian authors, however, the term has resonances of 'affective prayer' and a 'return to the heart', the same theme we explored in Chapter 2. We can accordingly give a working definition of *recogimiento* as 'an experiential tasting of God through contemplation'. Of particular importance to this nascent movement at the beginning of the sixteenth century were the reforms initiated within the Franciscan movement. These reforms found expression in a series of remarkable spiritual manuals beginning with the Seville edition of the *Obras de Bonaventura* of 1497 followed by the *Incendium Amoris* and *Liber meditationum* from the presses of the Abbey of Montserrat in Catalonia. Subsequently we find editions of St Augustine, St Bernard and Richard of St Victor rapidly being produced. In the *Exercitatorio de la Vida Espiritual* of 1500 (the *Spiritual Exercises*), written by García de Cisneros (another of this first wave of spiritual classics), we find the first written definition of the 'prayer of recollection': 'Recollect yourself often from low things to high, from temporal to eternal, from exterior to interior, from vain things to those that endure.'[3]

As this form of affective or 'recollected' prayer emerges in early modern Spain we see the influence of a whole range of authors, in particular from the Dionysian and Victorine schools and the Franciscan reformers of the late fifteenth century.[4] One such description of this type of prayer is to be found in the *Tercer Abecedario/Third Spiritual Alphabet* of the Franciscan friar Francisco de Osuna (1527) which would subsequently have such a powerful effect on the spiritual development of the young Teresa of Avila.

This chapter will concentrate on the form of contemplative practice described in these early Iberian authors before moving on, in Chapter 4, to a closer examination of the work of St Teresa of Avila and St John of the Cross. As we survey these forms of prayer I will argue that they possess a family resemblance to the Buddhist notions of *sati* already surveyed and the emerging notion of mindfulness as understood in the present secular Western setting. I will argue that the Iberian authors reference this spiritual practice by using the term *oración mental* which is normally translated into English by the term 'mental prayer'. In describing these practices I want to suggest that 'mindfulness', as recently rediscovered in the Anglophone world, would not be entirely inappropriate as a translation for this term. However, as stated earlier, I think the Christian prayer tradition is best understood as a dialogue of head and heart – it is not simply cognitive as some of the contemporary strands of mindfulness suggest. In this respect I am not making a case for *sati*/mindfulness as 'bare attention': the Christian way of mindfulness is a Prayer of the Heart, a form of 'heartfulness'.

Second, as I have already stated, in contrast to some of the Buddhist and psychological models of mindfulness, the Christian path is one that clearly acknowledges the transcendental/transpersonal within the human personality. Christian prayer/mindfulness can be distinguished from Buddhist prayer in that for the Christian there is always a transcendental perspective on the soul. With these two caveats in mind let us turn to our Iberian conversation partners.

The 'training of the heart' in the school of Abbot Cisneros

García Jiménez de Cisneros (1455–1510) was the cousin of the Spanish Patriarch Cardinal Francisco Jiménez de Cisneros, and Abbot of Montserrat (by command of the Catholic Monarchs) from 1493 to 1510. As mentioned, his *Exercitatorio de la vida espiritual* was first published in 1500 by the presses of Montserrat, along with his *Directorio de las Horas Canónicas*, and is seen now as one of the harbingers of that great spring flowering of Spanish mystical writing in the 'Golden Age' of the sixteenth century.[5] In as far as it is referred to today, it is in the context of the young Iñigo de Loyola who stayed in the environs of the abbey for some months before he made his way to the Holy Land after his conversion.

Like many of his contemporaries, Cisneros was wonderfully eclectic in his range of sources for this book of *Exercises*. As well as material from St Bonaventure (*De Triplici Via, Soliloquium de quatuor mentalibus exercitiis*) and other Franciscan sources such as Francesc Eiximenis' *Tractat de contemplació* and Carthusian sources such as Hugh of Balma's *Viae Lugent Sion*, he draws liberally on the work of the former Chancellor of the University of Paris, Jean Gerson, whom he refers to by name over 50 times (primarily drawing on the *Mountain of Contemplation*). Of the 69 chapters of the *Exercitatorio*, O'Reilly (1973), following Barault (1967), identifies 15 taken from Zutphen (seven from *De reformation virium animae* and eight from *De spiritualibus ascensionibus*), one from Thomas à Kempis' *Hortus rosarum* and 11 from Mombaer's *Rosetum* (whom Cisneros met in Paris in 1496). This is supplemented by material from the recent books of *devotio moderna* then popular on the Iberian peninsula, including passages from Ludolph of Saxony's *Vita Christi* (which was to so influence Loyola) and the work of Nicholas Kempf (*Alphabetum divini amoris* – usually attributed at this time to Gerson).[6]

In chapters 8 and 9 of the *Exercitatorio* we find Cisneros' first instructions on *oración mental* as a means towards the 'training of the heart': '*de exercitar su coraçón/exerceat cor suam*'. The nascent Spanish movement of affective prayer at the beginning of the sixteenth century was an entirely democratic one. Cisneros may have been a monk writing in the lofty fastnesses of Montserrat, but he is very insistent that the prayer techniques being taught were for everyone – not just religious and monastics. As he stresses in chapter 32:

> Thus we have seen that just because a person is simple it doesn't mean that the contemplative life is forbidden to them; for, we have seen, and still do see by experience, devout hermits, and some women draw more profit from this contemplative life and grow to love God more deeply than many important clergy and learned religious folk (*grandes clérigos y religiosos letrados*). (*Exercitatorio* 32.33–8, p. 278)[7]

The seeker, he suggests, often commences on the road to contemplation in a state of confusion and disturbed mind. He gives an accurate portrayal of this in chapter 39:

> At times it comes to pass that a man is alone in the body and withdrawn from the company of others, yet none the less he suffers phantasies, cogitations and melancholia (*fantasias, cogitaciones y malenconías*), and finds within himself most heavy and burdensome company. And such phantasies engender in him delirium and turmoil and cause him to speak much and be garrulous within his understanding. For the eyes of his understanding see first one thing and afterwards another: now they are led to the kitchen, now to the market: before them are brought carnal and unclean delights, dances, songs, beauties and such like vanities. (*Exercitatorio* 39.10–18, p. 298)

The *oración mental* will thus be the means whereby the heart 'like an unstable ship, tossed hither and thither on the waves, occupying itself in diverse affections and meditations (*affectos y meditaciones*)' (*Exercitatorio* 68.74–6, p. 436) will be brought to harbour. This recollection, conducted in a secret and quiet place, will thus calm the heart and make the seeker ready to enter the greater mysteries of the proposed contemplative path.[8] Its fruits, he suggests, comprise a more stable self (*Exercitatorio*

3.21, p. 102), a dissociation from distracting thoughts (3.31, p. 102), fervour ('fervor' – here we are close to the 'ardency' of the Buddhist *ātāpi* 3.45, p. 102), self-knowledge ('conoscimiento' – again reminiscent of the Buddhist *sampajañña* discussed earlier) and, finally, progress and merit on the spiritual path.

However, in contrast to the earlier Buddhist descriptions of *sati* we looked at, Cisneros, in common with Cassian and the desert elders, also stresses in chapter 8 that the aim of his programme is to 'soar to heaven with enkindled desire'.[9] This notion of the ascent of the heart to God is one Cisneros takes from the medieval Dionysian tradition, often referring to Hugh of Balma's *Viae Sion Lugent* available in Iberia at this juncture under the translated title of *Sol de Contemplativos*. Hugh of Balma's *Viae Sion Lugent* adopts the twelfth-century innovations of the Victorines and Cistercians, especially in the incorporation of the affective into the Dionysian tradition as well as building on it to develop a very experiential understanding of the role of the affect (*affectus*) in the search for God. Although the text does not use Dionysius' *eros* by name it makes use of the affective erotic schemas of Gallus to make its point. Influenced by Gerson, this tradition will also influence Teresa by her reading of Francisco de Osuna (see Tyler 2017).[10]

In his work, Balma contrasts the 'human curiosity' or 'useless science' ('*relicta humana curiositate scientiae inutilis argumentorum et opinionum captiva*', Hugh of Balma: 3) that is the knowledge of 'philosophers, scholars and secular masters' (Hugh of Balma: 4), searching after new curiosities, proofs and ideas contained within the covers of 'sheepskin quartos' (Hugh of Balma: 2), with the *vera sapientia*, the 'true knowledge', that will be expounded in his pages. Crucially, this first type of knowledge does not allow the 'flaming affections of love' (*per flammigeras amoris adfectiones*) to reach the Creator. The second type of knowledge, the *vera sapientia* or, as he refers to it later, the *mystica theologia*/'mystical theology' (Hugh of Balma: 2), is the knowledge that arises from this flaming affection of love which inflames the affect (*affectus*) and enlightens the intellect (*intellectus*) (Hugh of Balma: 3). These 'fiery aspirations of love' raise the soul to God and true knowledge: 'very rapidly, quicker than can be thought, without any prior or concomitant thought (*cogitation*), whenever she pleases, hundreds or thousands of times both day and night, the soul is drawn to possess God alone through countless yearning desires' (Hugh of Balma: 5).

Cisneros on Dionysius and Balma

Cisneros develops these Balmerian/Dionysian notions of the fiery ascent of the soul to God in chapter 28 of the *Exercitatorio* onwards: 'How the soul is lifted to God through quick and fervent love.'[11] Following Balma we have here an essentially Dionysian spiritual anthropology. Up to now, he says, he has described how the 'intellectus' (*entendimiento*) has been transformed by meditation and prayer – in particular, 'the firing of divine desire within the soul' (*desideria ignite ignis divini amoris est accendendus*) (*Exercitatorio* 28.6–7, p. 257). Yet from this point onwards the soul is raised to God not through 'any labour of the understanding' (*sin ninguna obra del entendimiento* 28.10, p. 258), for, as St Dionysius says, 'the wisdom is known by means of our ignorance, for no reasoning or understanding or human knowledge can raise the exercitant to a union after this manner' (28.12–14, p. 258).[12] Thus, the intellect and 'mental capacities' are insufficient to allow the soul to reach God – we need another capacity, which is why I have preferred the term 'mindfulness' (or even 'heartfulness') rather than 'mental prayer' as a translation of Cisneros' *oración mental*. Quoting Dionysius again, he states that this wisdom 'which attains to God' is not possible by 'wearying itself in speculations concerning Him or in thinking of Him in any lofty speculative manner whatsoever, unless this awakens love' (28.40–2, p. 259).[13] For, 'no tongue can describe it as the whole work is a purely spiritual one' (28.53–4, p. 258).[14]

To conclude his chapter, Cisneros stresses how such contemplation, by circumventing the intellect, makes it ideally suited to any manner of person 'however simple, whether an agricultural worker or a simple old woman' (*labrador o una sinple vegezuela*, 28.56/57, p. 258) who by this procedure 'may be quickly changed into a wise disciple', thus confirming the connection in Cisneros' thought between the availability of recollected *oración mental* and the wider accessibility of the fruits of this prayer to all seekers, not just those in monasteries and cloisters. In this respect, the prayer anticipates the wider democratic changes of the Reformation that will overtake the Western Church later in the sixteenth century – and even the resurgence in general interest in mindfulness practices in our own time.

In summary, following writers such as Balma we thus see in Cisneros a clear statement of *oración mental* not as a process of refining the intellect (*entendimiento* or *pensamiento*) but rather of going 'under the radar' of thought by means of contemplative exercises. The seeker engages in a process akin to *sati* whereby they observe the rising and falling of the thoughts as a means leading to the quietening of the heart.

Bernabé de Palma

Before we turn our gaze upon St Teresa of Avila and St John of the Cross, whose contributions to the history of Christian meditation are so important that it will be necessary to devote a separate chapter to each of them, I want to say a few words about another writer of this period who, like Cisneros, has been sadly neglected in the Anglophone literature on this area. From the point of view of the present work, Bernabé de Palma (1469–1532) is important not just because, again like Cisneros, he is one of the key writers of the early period of the Spanish Golden Age of writing on prayer (and will influence, among others, Teresa of Avila), but also because in his writings he quite explicitly uses the term *oración mental* to refer to the type of prayer that later writers will often term 'recollection/ *recogimiento*'. If we examine Palma's use of the term *oración mental* we find evidence that this term was being used at this period in a way not dissimilar to our contemporary uses of 'mindfulness', making my translation of that term in later writers such as Teresa and John more plausible.

From the point of view of the present interest in mindfulness it is worth noting that Palma himself, by trade a gardener, was not ordained a priest but worked as a third-order Franciscan having taken the habit in 1491 at the age of 22.[15] His most important and enduring work is the *Via Spiritus/The Spiritual Way*, which was published two months after his death in October 1532. It proved immensely popular and went through seven editions published in full in Seville (1532), Flanders (1533-4), Salamanca (1541) and Barcelona (1549), and in annotated form in Valencia (1546) and Toledo (1550 and 1553), before being placed on the infamous Valdés Index of 1559.[16]

Palma gives his fullest definition of *oración mental* in a series of Questions and Answers appended to the end of the treatise, this one being the answer to Question Nine, 'What exactly is the mental exercise of prayer?'[17] Here he describes the *ejercicio mental* as 'an internal reasoning in order to seek knowledge of God and of ourselves'.[18] This 'internal reasoning', much like the mindfulness we explored earlier, is to be sought in all manners of life and in all occupations; indeed, he gives us the striking analogy that mental prayer is as necessary to acquire 'friendship with the divine' (*amistad divinal*) as iron is for the blacksmith to forge his creations (p. 99). To illustrate this point, Palma gives a meditation on the origins of the bread that we eat not dissimilar to the 'raisin meditations' so familiar to those who embark upon MBSR or MBCT programmes. For in considering the bread we eat, he suggests, we contemplate the powers that have gone into the production of the wheat as it grew in the field and absorbed sun, earth and rain (p. 98). We are mindful then of God's actions in all things that surround us and all things can be the basis of this mindful contemplation. In chapter 5 of the Third Part of the book he stresses how we must seek the Spirit in all things, in all the shapes and forms of creation (p. 53). We must '*mira con atención*' – regard with attention – not only the world around us, but our own thoughts and contemplations. This, he says, will lead to what he calls here the '*quietud interior*' ('interior quiet', p. 53), and at other times the *sosiego* (peace or calm) that the soul seeks. Such contemplation will lead to what he calls an 'emptying of oneself' (*vacar*) as the *oración mental* leads us from mental preoccupation to centring upon the heart: 'This exercise is called mindfulness (*oración mental*) because the operations happen in the mind. It is a fitting and perfect way to come to the love of God and to look down upon ourselves, for by continuing this meditation we are set on fire to love Him' (chapter 4, p. 10).

In its unregarded state the mind is, he says, a source of disturbance (*turbación*) (chapter 4, p. 47) which in itself can lead us to doubt that we can ever find the calm we seek. For, he says, we must 'watch over our thoughts for just as two people cannot sit on a chair, so in the heart there cannot be attention and love of God and of the world' (p. 72). Focusing too much on our outer senses will lead us to neglect the heart and the spirit. At the heart of the self and spirit Palma stresses the incomprehensibility of God (p. 67), here reflecting the Dionysian/Balmian tradition that we saw Cisneros drawing upon above. It also connects to perhaps the most controversial aspect of Palma's teaching, which was probably why it fell foul of the Inquisitors in the middle of the sixteenth century: his insistence that mindfulness will lead to 'annihilation of the self'. As he states in chapter 3 of Part One of the text, 'many and diverse things are necessary in the building of the spiritual temple. But the first is the annihilation in our nothingness (*aniquiliación de nuestro nada*, p. 30)' arising from 'an emptying or knowledge of the nothingness that you are' (*un vaciamiento o conocimiento de la nada que eras*). This consideration of our nothingness is the surest way, he states, to achieve the 'inner calm' (*sosiego interior*) that he urges us to seek (p. 31). Palma's writing here, especially in his answers to Question Six, 'What manner do we adopt in the exercise of annihiliation?' (pp. 94–5), stresses that we can only come to the love of God by complete annihilation of all thoughts and senses – and in many respects his descriptions come close to some notions of 'non-self' found in Buddhism and to which we made reference earlier. By emphasizing the annihilation of the self and our nothingness, Palma pushes the possibilities of Christian mindfulness further than those who will follow him such as Teresa and John. Ultimately, however, for Palma, we should be guided in our meditations and prayers (as also stated by his contemporary Ignatius of Loyola) by the effects that our practices are having on our general mental and spiritual state.

As he says in Question Eleven, 'On the General Form of Prayer' (pp. 108–9), we are following God's will and advancing in meditation when we experience 'a softness which satisfies the understanding' (*una suavidad que satisface el entendimiento*); this, he emphasizes, is a clear signal that it is from God (p. 109). The contrary movement of hardness of heart and disturbance in the understanding, with increased attachment to consolations from the world of the senses, suggests we are deviating on our path – a process of 'discernment' very close to that later adopted by St Ignatius of Loyola in his *Spiritual Exercises*.

In summary, what we find in Palma is a striking account of mindfulness as a general means to acquiring the peace and virtues that he claims as the birthright of every Christian. As with so many of the Iberian writers (including, as we shall see, Teresa and John), Palma is light on the mechanics and wherefores of practising the art of meditation – this is certainly no Buddhist or modern mindfulness manual on the methods of meditation. However, where his writing appears so strikingly modern is in his emphasis on self-introspection, stillness and distrust of the 'monkey mind' as we seek a deeper peace; for him, this is found in the annihilation of the self and concentration on the *Nada*, which we will return to in Chapter 4 when we consider the work of St John of the Cross. Before we do that, however, it is necessary to introduce one of the most significant influences and teachers of John: his co-worker and spiritual master, St Teresa of Avila.

Influences on St Teresa of Avila

Writing several decades later than Cisneros and Palma, Teresa shared many of the influences that had shaped their spirituality, although it is unlikely that she would have read Cisneros' work itself.[19] However, like her fellow authors, she preferences an affective prayer that we could class under our earlier general heading of *recogimiento*. Just as Cisneros had been influenced by the Victorine Dionysianism of Balma, so Teresa found her inspiration in the *Third Spiritual Alphabet* of Palma's fellow Franciscan Francisco de Osuna, given to her by a wise uncle when she stumbled along the spiritual path as a young nun (see Tyler 2013).

Central to Osuna's affective theology in *The Third Spiritual Alphabet* is the notion of 'taste' of God rather than knowledge. In many passages he plays on the word *saber* ('know') and *sabor* ('taste') much as we will later see Teresa does. In Osuna's words, the 'mystical theology'[20] is a *sabroso saber* – literally, a 'tasty knowledge':

> They also call this type of prayer 'wisdom' because, as you can see, it is a tasty knowledge (*sabroso saber*); such knowledge, according to Saint Paul, is only found amongst the perfect, for the imperfect are not given such tasty morsels or such high doctrine (*tan buen manjar*). And it is called 'wisdom' for through it people will know how to taste God (*saben los hombres a qué sabe Dios*); of which taste the Wise Man says when he speaks of God: He gave wisdom to those who worked mercifully. (Osuna 6.2)[21]

Osuna, following the medieval tradition, named this type of theology the 'mystical theology' as opposed to what the scholastics called 'speculative theology' – akin to what is taught in most Western universities today under the term 'theology'. For Osuna, and later Teresa, the 'mystical theology' is thus a way of 'tasty knowing':

> [Theology] has two forms: one is called 'speculative' or 'investigative', which is the same thing, the other is called 'hidden', which is treated of here and which gives the title to this Third Alphabet. I do not presume to teach it here, as no mortal can, for Christ alone reserves this teaching only for himself, in secret and in the hearts in which this hidden theology dwells as divine science and something much more excellent than the other theology of which I spoke first ... This theology (the mystical theology) is said to be more perfect and better than the first, so says Gerson, as the first serves as an introduction leading to the second. (Osuna 6.2)[22]

Such direct experiential 'mystical theology' is clearly what appealed to Teresa, and she was to make this her own in works such as the famous Book of the Life/*El Libro de la Vida*.

Oración mental in Teresa's writings[23]

Teresa's first account of *oración mental* in her writings comes in an extended account in *The Life*, chapters 8 to 10. Here she contrasts the peace she receives from this activity with the 'war so troublesome' where she would frequently 'fall and rise' (*The Life* 8.2, *con estas caídas y con levantarme*) as her passions came and left her. In her last work, *The Interior Castle*, she brilliantly describes such thoughts:

> We shall always be glancing around and saying: 'Are people looking at me or not?' 'If I take a certain path shall I come to

any harm?' 'Dare I begin such and such a task?' 'Is it pride that is impelling me to do this?' 'Can anyone as wretched as I engage in so lofty an exercise as prayer?' 'Will people think better of me if I refrain from following the crowd?' 'For extremes are not good' they say, 'even in virtue; and I am such a sinner that if I were to fail I should only have farther to fall; perhaps I shall make no progress and in that case I shall only be doing good people harm; anyway, a person like myself has no need to make herself singular!' (*The Interior Castle* 1.2.10)[24]

This is as good a description as any of the 'monkey mind'[25] of the Buddhists – and that which contemporary practices of mindfulness seek to bring into stability by means such as awareness exercises. From the very beginning of her writing career Teresa is aware of this internal conflict between stabilized awareness of 'the heart' and the need to work with distracting *pensamiento*.

Her practice of contemplation, she says, 'drew her to the harbour of salvation' (*a puerto de salvación*, *The Life* 8.4). She refers to it here and later as her '*trato con Dios*: *Que no es otra cosa oración mental, a mi parecer, sino tratar de amistad, estando muchas veces tratando a solas con quien sabemos nos ama*' ('For mindfulness is none other, it appears to me, than a close intercourse, frequently practised on an intimate basis, with the one we know loves us').[26] The pivotal word here is '*trato*' – a difficult one to translate.

Where Teresa's method of prayer differs so clearly from the Buddhist mindfulness detailed above is the role that visualization and symbolic representation of Christ plays in her meditations.[27] However, where Teresa's account of mindfulness converges with the Buddhist accounts we explored in the earlier chapters is in the importance of drawing attention away from intellectual and mental activity to the location of what she calls 'the heart'. This, as with Palma, is not an anti-intellectual move but rather a consequence of the strategy of the medieval mystical theology to which she is heir. To overcome the whirring discourse of the intellect we will need to concentrate on the mindful *trato* with the beloved. This is why I feel the term 'mental prayer' can be misleading and why I prefer 'mindfulness' or even, as I said earlier, 'heartfulness', as a translation of *oración mental*. 'Mental' seems to have the contemporary association with the mind and cognitive activity whereas, I would like to suggest, Teresa is advocating something closer to the Buddhist practice of mindfulness outlined above, and certainly closer to the contemporary practice of mindfulness discussed by commentators such as Jon Kabat-Zinn. As she says later in chapter 13: 'therefore it is of great importance, when we begin to practise prayer, not to be intimidated by thoughts, and believe you me, for I have had experience of this' (*The Life* 13.7).[28] Or, as she later puts it in chapter 17, rather poetically translated by Matthew, the thoughts are like 'unquiet little Gnatts, which buzze, and whizze by night, heer and there, for just so, are these Powers wont to goe, from one to another' (*The Life* 17.6).[29]

In summary, then, from these passages I think a strong case can be made to regard Teresa's *oración mental* as closer to the contemporary notion of mindfulness, or 'heartfulness' (both terms convey, I would argue, the studied imprecision that Teresa is aiming at), in the fashion described by Cisneros and Palma. In the descriptions above what clearly differentiates Teresa's approach is the necessary connection between her own mindful prayer and attention in meditation to the person of Christ. Yet where she comes close to the Buddhist masters is her challenge to the discursive power of the intellect and the necessary use of symbol and image to allow this power to be 'short-circuited' to allow direct awareness of self and indeed all creation around (*The Life* 9.5). In consequence, I don't think it is far-fetched to talk of Teresa, in the early stages at least, as advocating a practice of 'mindfulness or heartfulness' as she refashions and makes her own the tradition of *recogimiento* to which she is heir. We shall return to her discourse in Chapter 4 where we shall spell out the consequences of her treatment for contemporary practitioners of mindfulness.

Conclusions

I have argued in this chapter that the Spanish term *oración mental*, as used by the authors of the Spanish Golden Age such as Cisneros, Palma and Teresa, would be better understood from the present context as a cousin to the Buddhist mindfulness. I would go so far as to preference the term 'mindfulness' or 'heartfulness' as a translation of the term into English and this is the translation I shall adopt for the rest of this book. My reasons can be summarized as follows:

First, as used in the contemplative schemas of Cisneros, Palma and Teresa it is not fanciful to see it described as a process of 'mindful attention' – particularly to what they term 'the heart' as a means of circumventing the action of the mind (the monkey mind). Rather they are suggesting a means (following Dionysius) of 'learned ignorance' whereby the cognitive faculties are quietened as 'the soul' is drawn to an experiential awareness of the Divine.

Second, the current obsession with the 'mental' creates a too cognitive resonance that is not the intention of the authors; rather, they want to move away from the head to the heart.

For the reasons given it is possible to scope an understanding of *sati* that is as much heartfulness as mindfulness: indeed, its link to the Sanskrit *smṛti* suggests a 'family resemblance' to the recollection/*recogimiento* of the Spanish school.

Like the Buddha, Cisneros in particular stresses that we must not engage in useless speculation on the nature of the Godhead but rather engage simply in contemplation for contemplation's sake. His notion of mental prayer is very democratic. As he concludes in the *Exercitatorio*: 'many who live in the world and have sufficient time, leisure, knowledge and talent to devote themselves wholly to God [should have] faith, hope and charity for there is no great instruction for them to seek, by engaging in profound study, that they may devote all their affection to God' (*Exercitatorio* 67.49–55, p. 433). This attitude has resonances with the contemporary 'lay' rediscovery of mindfulness as contemplative practice. As Teresa puts it in *The Way of Perfection*, the path of *oración mental* is as much for 'the unskilled peasant boy' as 'the wisest and most learned of men' (chapter 22) and Palma emphasizes how the practice of mindfulness can take place in any aspect of our daily lives.

In an essay comparing the path of the *Cloud of Unknowing* with the Buddhist Dhamma, Rupert Gethin concludes that both traditions 'present the contemplative path, the path of purification, as a turning away from ordinary discursive thought by means of techniques of simplifying and emptying the mind'.[30] By such means, Gethin suggests, the 'heart' of the seeker is profoundly restructured by engaging in contemplative practices. If, as I have argued, Teresa, Palma and Cisneros are likewise inviting us to engage in this move away from the abstractions of the intellect to the heart of spiritual transformation then it seems that their term for this process – *oración mental* – will be better conveyed to a contemporary Anglophone audience by 'heartfulness' or 'mindfulness' rather than the cognitive 'mental prayer'.

Having established my reasons for preferring the term 'mindfulness' as a translation of *oración mental* in the Spanish tradition we shall stay with this tradition in the next chapter as we explore the implications of Teresa's and John's understanding of the term for contemporary spiritual seekers.

Exercise Three: Sacred Breath

> *The Lord God formed man from the dust ... and breathed [into him] the breath of life.* (Genesis 2.7)

All breath is sacred and the words we associate with mind, soul and psyche usually have their origins from words for breath, air and breathing. The English word 'soul', like the German *Seele*, has roots in the Gothic *saiwala* and Old German *saiwalô*, which can be linked with the Greek *aiolos*: mobile, coloured, iridescent, and also the mythical keeper of the Winds.[31] The Greek word *psyche* – from which words such as 'psychology' and 'psychotherapy' are derived – has links with the Greek word *psykhein*, 'to blow, cool', as well as various terms for life-force, ghost, spirit and even butterfly. The Latin word for soul, *animus* – the source of words such as 'animate' – is related to the Greek *anemos*/'wind or breeze' and possibly the Sanskrit *ānila*/'air, wind' and is cognate with the Old Irish *anal*, Welsh *anadl*/'breath' and Old Irish *animm*/'soul'.

Thus, throughout different cultures and times breath and the soul/psyche have been inextricably linked. So too in meditation, the importance of breath-awareness has been continually emphasized.

So let us begin our exercise by once again composing the time and place, preparing ourselves for the task ahead and putting ourselves once again in the presence of the mystery of our being: feet on the floor, bottom on the ground, back straight.

Make yourself comfortable and now give yourself ten minutes to be aware of your breath. Again, this is a simple exercise that requires simple concentration on the breath as it occurs. First, spend some time becoming aware of the body as in the previous exercise. Now, first notice the gentle rising and falling of the chest. Do not try to alter the rhythm of the breathing, just be aware of it as it occurs and the sensation in your chest as it rises and falls. Now notice the gentle sensations as the cold air enters your nostrils. Follow it through as it moves down into your lungs. Concentrate on the warm air that you breathe out. Again, notice where it is coming from. As the exercise continues concentrate on one spot, in the nostrils, on the lips, in the chest, and be aware of the rhythm of breath as you inhale and exhale.

o O o

Again this is a deceptively simple exercise that can have powerful repercussions. It is surprising how much we take the ubiquitous process of breathing for granted – our faithful companion is very under-appreciated! Unlike some advanced meditation/mindfulness exercises, this one does not call for a manipulation of breath and such concentrated breath awareness is best confined to these short periods rather than enforced for hours on end. However, its short-term effects can be very peaceful and life-enhancing.

Variations on the Exercise

From a Christian point of view this exercise can be very rewarding. As well as the reminder from the Genesis creation story with which we began, it is noticeable how often Jesus will use breath to communicate with his followers. As is written in John's Gospel:

> When it was evening on that day, the first day of the week, and the doors of the house ... were locked for fear ... Jesus came and stood among them and said, 'Peace be with you ... As the Father has sent me, so I send you.' When he had said this, he breathed on them and said to them, 'Receive the Holy Spirit ...' (John 20.19–22)

So, a variation of the breathing exercise, which we will return to in the next chapter, is to repeat the name of Jesus with each breath. Or, to inhale the breath of the Holy Spirit with each breath while releasing all that binds us and confuses us with the out-breath.

The Indian mystic Sri Aurobindo follows Indian tradition in reflecting on five aspects of breath, or *Prāna*. There is the inhalation that is the Life-breath and brings life into us. Then there is the *Apana* or breath of death that originates in the lower part of the body and will expel our final breath when we expire. The third, *Samana*, regulates these two and occurs midway in the chest. *Vyana*, the fourth, distributes the vital energies throughout the body, and finally *Udana*, the fifth, moves the breath from the body to the crown of the head and is our means of communicating with the transcendent realm (Sri Aurobindo 1994, p. 115). We can refine the breathing exercise by spending time concentrating on any one of these, or tracing their movement through our body.

Notes

1 Montserrat, July 2017.
2 My translation.
3 'Recolígete muchas vezes de las cosas baxas a las altas. De las temporales a las eternas. De las exteriores a las interiores. De las vanas a las que siempre han durar' (p. 452, 69.133–5).
4 For more on this tradition, see Tyler 2011.
5 I shall use the edition in the *Obras Completas* edited by Dom Cipriano Baraut (Montserrat, 1965). Although I shall mainly make my own translations of the Catalan and Latin versions, I have consulted Allison Peers's 1929 translation of the Catalan text and that of the 'Monk of St Augustine's Monastery' (1876) of the Latin text. I shall give page number, paragraph and chapter from Baraut's edition for each citation. For more on the relationship between Loyola and Cisneros, see my chapter 'Mystical Desire: St Ignatius of Loyola and Affective Dionysianism', in *Id Quod Volo: The Dynamics of Desire in the Spiritual Exercises and Postmodernity*, ed. J. Hanvey and T. La Couter, Brill, forthcoming.
6 For more on the wider influences on Cisneros, see O'Reilly 1973, Baraut 1967 and Melloni 2000.
7 I have argued elsewhere that here, as in so much, Cisneros is heavily influenced by the work of Jean Gerson (see Tyler 2017).
8 Again, like Origen quoted earlier, Cisneros is remarkably flexible in the methods he prescribes. The seeker may adopt the bodily posture for prayer that they find most agreeable (he suggests many).
9 'Por desseos ençendidos al çielo/ cum anima ignitis desideriis in celum conatur ascendere.'
10 Balma's work belongs to that same strand of European medieval thought that influenced the English author of *The Cloud of Unknowing*. Unfortunately lack of space here means that we cannot devote much time to that other great 'manual of mindfulness'. However, for more on the interrelationship between the two, see my 'The Carthusians and the *Cloud of Unknowing*', in *The Oxford Handbook to Dionysius the Areopagite*, ed. M. Edwards, D. Pallis and G. Steiris, Oxford University Press (forthcoming).
11 The Catalan version is '*Cómo nuestro pensamiento se levanta en dios por bivo y ardiente amor (sin algún conosciento del entendimiento, ni de otra cosa alguna)*', causing Allison Peers to translate 'how our thought is lifted up to God'. I prefer 'soul' to 'thought' as a translation for the reasons set out in Tyler 2016, especially the final chapter.
12 '*Ninguna razón ni entendimiento ni conoscimiento humano/ nulla humana ratio, intellectus vel noticia elevat animam.*'

13 'Quod non speculatur vel considerat eum speculative vel subtiliter, quod quidem non movet ad amorem.'

14 'Por ninguna lengua, ca todo esto es pura obra spiritual.'

15 For this account of Palma's background, I am largely referring to that given by Martín in his 1998 edition of the *Via Spiritus/The Spiritual Way*.

16 For more on this Index and its influence on Spanish mystical writing, see Tyler 2011 and 2013.

17 I will use Martín's 1998 edition of the *Via Spiritus/The Spiritual Way* with my own translations.

18 '*Interiormente raciocinando buscar el conocimiento de Dios y de nosotros mismos*' (p. 98).

19 Although she makes reference to the work of Osuna and his Franciscan contemporary Bernardo de Laredo, there is no direct reference to Palma. However, the possibility that she was familiar with his work cannot be ruled out as she refers to her acquaintance with the books of popular spirituality then being circulated several times in her writings – such as in *The Book of the Life*.

20 In this respect Osuna is following the medieval Victorines and Gerson in their distinction between the *vera sapientia* (that is, the mystical theology) and the 'useless scientific curiosity' of the intellectual mind, as described above. See also Tyler 2011.

21 '*Llámese también esta manera de oración sabiduría, que, según viste, es sabroso saber; la cual sabiduría dice San Pablo que hablaba entre los perfectos solamente, porque a los imperfectos no les daba tan buen manjar ni tan alta doctrina. Y dícese sabiduría porque mediante ella saben los hombres a qué sabe Dios; donde de aquésta dice el Sabio hablando de Dios: A los que piadosamente obran dio la sabiduría.*' Mary Giles writes in her translation of this passage (Osuna 1981, p. 164): 'Osuna's play on the word "saber" which means both "to know" and "to taste" defies translation.'

22 '*La cual aún es en dos maneras: una se llama especulativa o escudriñadora, que es el mismo, y otra escondida, que es la que se trata o a la que se intitula este tercero alfabeto; no que en él presuma yo enseñarla, pues ninguno de los mortales la enseñó, porque Christo guardó para sí este oficio de enseñar en secreto a los corazones en que viviese aquesta teología escondida como ciencia divina y mucho más excelente que la otra teología de que hablamos primer ... Esta teología se dice más perfecta o mejor que la primera, según dice Gersón, porque de la primera como de un principio se servir.*'

23 In my desire to go back to Teresa's original voice I have worked with the closest edition to Teresa's original, that edited by Efrén de la Madre de Dios and Otger Steggink in the *Obras Completas de Santa Teresa de Jésus* (St Teresa in the series Biblioteca de Autores Cristianos,

Madrid, Biblioteca de Autores Cristianos, 1997). As the first full English translations of her work by Kavanaugh and Rodriguez and Allison Peers rely heavily on the older critical edition by P. Silverio de Santa Teresa, I have also turned to this edition for certain passages as published in *Santa Teresa Obras Completas* edited by Tomás Alvarez in the edition of *Monte Carmelo* (Alvarez 1998). All bibliographical details for these works can be found in the Bibliography. Unless stated, all translations of Teresa's works are my own.

24 I have used Allison Peers's translation here as he brings out perfectly Teresa's sense of an 'inner dialogue' that proceeds in the mind of one starting out on a path of prayer or contemplation.

25 Or as Teresa calls it poetically in *The Book of the Life* 15.6: 'the grinding mill of the intellect' – *moledor entendimiento*. In the same passage she also refers to 'restless bees' that 'gad about' (Matthew's translation).

26 Again, a tricky passage to translate and preserve the sense of intimacy Teresa wants to convey here. Allison Peers retains this sense with his translation: 'Mental prayer, in my view, is nothing but friendly intercourse, and frequent solitary converse, with Him Who we know loves us.' Kavanaugh and Rodriguez give a more distant: 'Mental prayer in my opinion is nothing less than an intimate sharing between friends; it means taking time frequently to be alone with Him who we know loves us.' Perhaps the intimacy we would experience with a boyfriend or girlfriend is suggested.

27 See, for example, *The Life* 9.1–4 and the beginning of her lengthy discourse in the *The Way of Perfection* on *oración mental* (chapter 22) where she points out how we must behave in such an encounter; we will return to this in the next chapter.

28 '*Ansí que va mucho a los principios de comenzar oración a no amilanar los pensamientos, y créanme esto, porque lo tengo por espieriencia.*'

29 '*Que no parece sino de estas maripositas de las noches, importunas y desasosegadas: ansí anda de un cabo a otro.*'

30 From 'Emptiness and Unknowing: An Essay in Comparative Mysticism', in *Studies in Early Buddhism in Memory of L. S. Cousins*, ed. P. Harvey and N. Appleton. London: Equinox, forthcoming.

31 For more on this, see Tyler 2016.

4

The Mindful Way – St Teresa of Avila and St John of the Cross

Caprimulgus

'Where have you fled my beloved?
I went out unseen,
And you were gone.'

My silent, night-screaming angels
Have departed.
What joy it was
To walk unseen into their embrace.

Now.
This cross-filled Spanish night,
Alone,
Points the way
From Avila to the stars.[1]

'A book of advice and counsel'

My intention is to suggest a few remedies for a number of temptations which come to those engaged on the religious path and to explain my intention in founding this house, that is, regarding the perfection that is observed here – over and above that observed in our Constitution – and to write of other things as the Lord reveals them to me and as they occur to me; since I do not know what I am going to say I cannot set it down in suitable order; and I believe it is better for me not to do so, for it is quite unsuitable that I should be writing in this way at all. May the Lord lay His hand on all that I do so that it may be in accordance with His holy will; this then is always my desire, although my works are as faulty as I *am*. (CE: Prologue 2)[2]

So begins the 'little book of advice and counsel' (the words are the saint's own) that Teresa wrote for her religious sisters sometime around 1566. The writing stands at a watershed in Teresa's life and she had recently celebrated her fiftieth birthday. Like so many who embark upon the spiritual path she had entered the convent (in her own words in the earlier *Book of the Life*) in something of a daze. Yes, she had been attracted to the order, harmony and peace of the life and the example of the older, wiser nuns she had met. However, she also brought into the convent something of the disturbance and colour of the vibrant sixteenth-century Castilian life within which she had been immersed for so many years. For some time she struggled to reconcile the various parts of her character and this all led to a sort of nervous, physical and spiritual breakdown experienced in her mid-thirties and described so vividly in the *Book of the Life* (see Tyler 2013, chapter 4). In the following years as she began to regain her composure, helped and assisted by spiritual direction both from within her family and from the wider Avilan religious community, she finally resolved that the way forward for herself, and other like-minded women, was to begin to found what she called her 'little dove-cotes': places of prayer and peace where small groups of sisters (around a dozen) could engage in a mindful path separated from the busy world around them. She founded the first such convent, San José, in Avila in 1562, moving there herself the following year for what she later called the most restful years of her life. In solitude and peace she began her career as a wordsmith. This began initially out of necessity as the books of prayer needed to encourage 'her daughters' – which she had read so avidly as a young woman, and which we described in the previous chapter – were now off-limits according to the Valdés Index of 1559. Accordingly, in order to inspire the sisters she began to write her own works of prayer beginning with the famous *Book of the Life*. As we have seen, this extraordinarily original work described the ups and downs of her spiritual path up to this point in her life, warts and all, including all the spiritual ecstasies and sweetnesses she had experienced in prayer (among which was the famous 'Transverberation of the Heart', immortalized in Bernini's statue of the 'Ecstasy of St Teresa' at Santa Maria della Vittoria in Rome). The new book that she completed after the *Book of the Life*, her little book of advice and counsel, was to be different. Here, in what has come to be called *The Way of Perfection* (not initially Teresa's title for the book), we find the more measured and mature reflections of one who has withstood the ups and downs of the spiritual life as lived in community and finally found what we heard her describe in the previous chapter as 'the harbours of peace'. Thus *The Way* is a more measured and peaceful text than its predecessor in that it does not so much concentrate on the peaks and troughs of the religious life – the ecstasies and dark nights she had described earlier – but rather on the ordinary everyday living-out of what we call in this book the path of mindfulness or, better, heartfulness. In this respect we can treat it as a manual for mindfulness from the Christian tradition that details how this form of prayer can be integrated into our ordinary everyday lives. Yes, Teresa primarily wrote for her sisters in religion, but this text was the only one she considered for wider publication in her lifetime and she even went so far as to prepare a text for publication – although this was not to happen until after her death; she was unhappy with the liberties taken by her (unknown) editor and this bowdlerized version never made it into wider circulation. As with so many of the Teresian texts we possess today, we have the editor of the first complete edition of her works, Fray Luis de León, to thank for the final version that he produced, where he sought to preserve the immediate spontaneity and freshness of Teresa's text. As in the quotation with which I began this chapter, we hear in Teresa's work a unique voice among spiritual writers that has gained for her a special place among her readers over the past five centuries – her works have never been out of print since Luis de León's first edition, and are translated into most of the world's languages. Her prose, with all its ellipses, false starts, inconsistencies and seeming contradictions, is the authentic voice of one who has toiled for long on the spiritual journey and finally received her rewards. I hope to try in small measure to reproduce something of this voice in the translations of her work into English for the present volume.[3]

It would be a mistake, then, to treat Teresa's *Way* as a prayer manual or set of instructions for achieving mindful states. Like all great writers on prayer, she respects the 'subtle nothingness' that lies at the heart of the contemplative life and realizes how difficult it is to place the gossamer-like warp and weft of prayer on to the written page. Her discursive style, often decried as an example of her lack of learning as a 'simple woman', is now accepted by many scholars as being a strategy she adopts to talk about the secret world of prayer while preserving respect for the mystery of the individual encounter with the Divine. Mindfulness or heartfulness is a personal journey that no one else can trespass upon. Teresa understands and respects this crucial truth while offering words of advice and encouragement from the sidelines. In such a spirit, I would argue, we must approach Teresa's manual of mindfulness – *The Way of Perfection*. Throughout, she emphasizes the healing metaphor introduced in the passage above for we embark upon the path of mindfulness and prayer in order to heal the soul. This, she stresses to her readers, is their *trato y lenguaje* – their business and language (CV: 20.4). Thus the path of mindfulness is as much about learning a new language as a new way of life.

Right disposition

Contemporary readers looking in *The Way* for a clear path of mindfulness will be disappointed. This is because Teresa also understands one of the key aspects of meditation that we heard expressed by John Cassian in an earlier chapter (an author she was not unfamiliar with; see CV: 19.13). As he expressed it: 'what we would like to be at the time of prayer, try to be outside of prayer'. For Teresa, as for Cassian, there is an essential link between our prayer lives and our 'ordinary everyday lives'. Indeed, as contemporary Buddhist masters such as the American Jack Kornfield and the Vietnamese Thich Nhat Hahn have pointed out (and to which we shall return later in this book), the search for a prayer-life somehow divorced from our everyday lives is ultimately doomed to failure. If we use prayer, meditation or mindfulness practices as means to run away or hide from the challenges of our daily lives, we shall ultimately be thwarted. In fact, our daily engagement with the rough and tumble of everyday life, as Teresa is the first to recognize, is possibly the best test for the effectiveness of the type of prayer and meditation we are developing. Thus, when we look at the structure of *The Way* we find that less than half of it is dedicated to what we would call prayer or mindfulness techniques. Rather, Teresa devotes the majority of the text to the art of developing a balanced life where we can harmonize the call of the Divine with our ordinary lives. This is what the Buddhists call the development of *Sila* or right morality. Likewise, for Teresa it is an essential foundation for the development of the Christian contemplative life – without it, she will argue, all will be lost. For Teresa the three qualities at the heart of the religious life are therefore: *love of neighbour*, *detachment* and *humility* (CV: 4.4)[4] and she will return to these three important aspects of *Sila* throughout the text.

As with so much writing on prayer, *love* lies at the heart of much of what she wants to write, as she states in the Prologue of *The Way* (CV: 3):

> I know that I am lacking neither in love nor in desire to do all I can to help the souls of my sisters to make great progress in the service of the Lord. It may be that this love, together with my years and the experience which I have of a number of convents, will make me more successful in writing about small matters than learned men can be ... I shall speak of nothing of which I have no experience, either in my own life

or in the observation of others, or which the Lord has not taught me in prayer.

She will teach us from her heart and her experience and, while not decrying the need for 'head knowledge', she stresses that her way of mindfulness, as we saw in Chapter 3, will be one that 'goes under the radar' of the intellect to find the heartfulness that lies at the foundation of our human selves.

The other danger she recognizes from the outset is that the life of prayer can lead to a cutting-off from the world around. One of the drawbacks of the present wave of mindfulness is the tendency towards its adoption as a privatized religion for the late capitalist world. Slavoj Žižek, the pungent Slovenian critic, describes it as ideally suited to the needs of the late capitalist world when he states: 'the "Western Buddhist" meditative stance is arguably the most effective way for us to fully participate in capitalist dynamics whilst retaining the semblance of mental health'.[5] The preponderance of mindfulness apps and online courses may lead to a privatization of prayer with little concern for its effects and relation to the world around us. From the outset Teresa is adamant in opposing this, stressing that we begin the life of prayer by asking ourselves how it may relate to and help bring peace to a world in need of healing, what she dramatically calls 'the world in flames':

> Oh, my sisters in Christ! Help me to entreat this of the Lord, Who has brought you together here for that very purpose. This is your vocation; this must be your business; these must be your desires; these your tears; these your petitions. Let us not pray for worldly things, my sisters. It makes me laugh, and yet it makes me sad, when I hear of the things which people come here to beg us to pray to God for; we are to ask His Majesty to give them money and to provide them with incomes – I wish that some of these people would entreat God to enable them to trample all such things beneath their feet. Their intentions are quite good, and I do as they ask because I

see that they are really devout people, though I do not myself believe that God ever hears me when I pray for such things. The world is in flames. (CV: 1.5)

Prayer (and mindfulness), as she points out, can so easily be twisted by the demands of the ego to our own ends rather than being a gateway to the Divine. Throughout the spiritual journey we must be on our guard against the subtle dangers and poison of the ego. Hence the necessity established very early on in the Christian tradition, that we investigated earlier, for the seeker to find someone to talk to – a prayer guide or soul companion – who can act as a foil to talk through these challenges and snares. For at the onset of our prayer journey, and at frequent intervals during it, we must ask ourselves, 'For whose end am I doing this?' If it is solely for my own pleasure, satisfaction and delight, then the project will be doomed from the start. Yes, there may be spiritual delights and sweetnesses on the way – perhaps even the ecstasies so many of the saints describe – yet to make this the goal of our prayer journey is to have missed the point from the start, for we will be setting ourselves up to fail. For this reason, as we have outlined, Teresa emphasizes from the beginning the three necessary conditions for mindfulness: love of neighbour, detachment and humility. These alone will provide the right conditions for the beginning of a prayer practice that will not later get caught up with serving the individual ego rather than freeing us to perceive the transcendent. As she states in the second chapter of *The Way* with her inimitable provocative humour:

> These arms [of humility and poverty] must appear on our banners and at all costs we must keep this rule – as regards our house, our clothes, our speech, and (which is much more important) our thoughts. So long as this is done, there need be no fear, with the help of God, that religious observances in this house will decline, for, as Saint Clare said, the walls of poverty are very strong ... Have a care to this, for the love

of God; and this I beg of you by His blood. If I may say what my conscience bids me, I should wish that, on the day when you build such edifices, they may fall down *and kill you all*. (CV/CE: 2.8)[6]

... It would hardly look well if the house of thirteen poor women made a great noise when it fell, for those who are really poor must make no noise: unless they live a noiseless life people will never take pity on them. (CV: 2.10)

Throughout her work she is concerned to stress that the two strongest poisons to the 'way of perfection' are riches and honour. The Spain of Teresa's day was obsessed with what was termed *honra* – even in the convents and monasteries one's place was determined by one's position in society and woe betide the person who sought to move 'above their station'. How easily the sensitive ego is slighted by offences to its honour and status. Likewise, the desire for material comfort and riches can act as a subtle poison to the spiritual path, leading us astray. Teresa's master, Fray Francisco de Osuna, began his 'Spiritual Alphabet' with the maxim: *anden siempre juntamente – la persona y espíritu* – 'always walking together the person and the spirit' (Osuna 1). We must maintain a congruence between our material and spiritual aspirations. Once one comes off track the other will inevitably suffer. In this vein Teresa stresses in chapter 4 of *The Way* the need for harmony between what she terms the interior and the exterior:

Before speaking of the interior life – that is, of prayer – I shall speak of certain things which those who attempt to walk along the way of prayer must of necessity practise. So necessary are these that, even though not greatly given to contemplation, people who have them can advance a long way in the Lord's service, while, unless they have them, they cannot possibly be great contemplatives, and, if they think they are, they are much mistaken. (CV: 4.3)

As human beings we walk a middle path between two extremes: either to over-spiritualize our lives or to become over-materialized. Each is equally dangerous. As we saw in an earlier chapter, Cassian quotes with approval the old Greek saying 'extremes meet' and Abba Poemen stressed that 'everything that goes to excess comes from the demons', whether this is excessive material indulgence or excessive unhinged piety. Detachment towards possessions, the constant search for humility and, most of all, love of neighbour should protect us from these two extremes.

Prayer, mindfulness and contemplation all thus require correct preparation. Again one of the dangers of the recent explosion of mindfulness practices is that such practices enacted without the necessary hinterland of preparation can sometimes lead to the opposite effects of what is intended. As we saw in a previous chapter, mindfulness or *sati* within Buddhist practice has a specific task to perform within a specific religious context. This is reflected in Teresa's path of mindfulness where the actions and behaviour we perform outside of the prayer sessions is as equally important as how we behave in prayer: 'what you would like to be in the time of prayer, try to be outside of prayer'. If we follow this advice then prayer will from the start be integrated into our whole lives and not be compartmentalized into a separate bubble. From this perspective, Teresa concludes the first part of *The Way* by comparing the person embarking upon the path of prayer and mindfulness to one playing a game of chess – a daring simile for a woman at this time (who were not meant to play such games, especially in convents) and one that was removed in the later edition of the book:

> I hope you do not think I have written too much about this already; for I have only been placing the board, as they say. You have asked me to tell you about the first steps in prayer; although God did not lead me by them, my daughters, I know no others, and even now I can hardly have acquired

these elementary virtues. But you may be sure that anyone who cannot set out the pieces in a game of chess will never be able to play well, and, if he does not know how to give check, he will not be able to bring about a checkmate. Now you will reprove me for talking about games, as we do not play them in this house and are forbidden to do so. That will show you what kind of a mother God has given you – she even knows about vanities like this! However, they say that the game is sometimes legitimate. How legitimate it will be for us to play it in this way, and, if we play it frequently, how quickly we shall give checkmate to this Divine King! He will not be able to move out of our check nor will He desire to do so. (CE: 16.1)

Oración mental/mindfulness

Having thus dealt with the preliminary conditions for prayer, Teresa now begins her exposition of what she calls the *oración mental* and which, following my argument in the previous chapter, I shall call mindfulness. As discussed in Chapter 3, an essential part of this practice for Teresa is its role in calming the churning sea of the mind. As she now puts it in *The Way*:

> There are some souls, and some intellects, as unruly as horses not yet broken in. No one can stop them: now they go this way, now that way; they are never still.[7]
> Some people are either like this by nature or God permits them to become so. I am very sorry for them; they seem to me like people who are very thirsty and see water a long way off, yet, when they try to go to it, find someone who all the time is barring their path – at the beginning of their journey, in the middle and at the end. (CV: 19.2)

Continuing the metaphor, mindfulness will thus be that which 'ties up' the intellect, so 'restraining the mind' as to allow prayer and contemplation to proceed: 'all who can walk along this road will walk restfully and securely, for one always walks restfully when the understanding is restrained' (CV: 19.1).[8] Yet, she stresses, we must not also make the quest for mindfulness an end in itself (this more than anything would distinguish what Teresa is advocating from some of the contemporary expositions of mindfulness we discussed earlier). For her, mindfulness, the stillness of the intellect through the focus on the heart, is a gift given by the Lord which we must wait for patiently. It is a condition to enable us to proceed in prayer (and will often make that journey easier), but not a *necessary* condition. Here she follows the great tradition of Christian spiritual writers stretching back to St Augustine who stress that the initiative for our prayer-life comes from the other, the Divine, not from ourselves. Indeed, as emphasized earlier, focus on prayer emanating from the ego will ultimately prove futile. The work begins and ends in the Divine, a theme we shall return to at the end of the chapter where we discuss the teaching of St Teresa's co-worker, St John of the Cross. For now she writes:

> O souls, who are not able to have much discourse of the understanding or hold your thoughts upon God without being distracted – get used to it! Get used to it! See, I know that you can do this: for I myself endured this trial of not being able to let the mind rest peacefully on one subject for many years – and a very hard trial it is – but I know the Lord does not leave us so abandoned; for if we approach Him with humility to accompany us He will not deny it and if a whole year passes without our obtaining it, it will come. I say this: it is possible to form the habit of walking at the side of this true Master. (CE: 42.2)[9]

The initiative will come from the Divine. For our part we must cultivate an atmosphere of peace within the soul whereby the Divine Lover can enter (a theme we shall return to later with St John of the Cross). These passages at the centre of *The Way* take us to the heart of Teresa's journey of mindfulness. And at the same time as they reveal her closeness to the Buddhist notions of *sati* we essayed in an earlier chapter, they also highlight the essential distinguishing mark of Teresa's mindful way – for her it is a way that must begin and end with the presence of the Divine Other: Jesus Christ. As she puts it in CV: 16.11: 'O Lord! All our trouble comes to us from not having our eyes fixed upon You. If we only looked at the way along which we are walking, we should soon arrive; but we stumble and fall a thousand times and stray from the way because, as I say, we do not set our eyes on the true Way.' And crucially at the beginning of chapter 26:

> Re-present the Lord Himself joined with you and see how lovingly and how humbly He is teaching you – and, believe me, you should stay with so good a Friend for as long as you can before you leave Him. If you become accustomed to having Him at your side, and if He sees that you love Him to be there and are always trying to please Him, you will never be able, as we put it, to send Him away, nor will He ever fail you. He will help you in all your trials and you will have Him everywhere. Do you think it is a small thing to have such a Friend as that beside you? (CV: 26.1)[10]

'*Representad al mismo Señor junto con vos*' – come into the *presence* of the Lord, make the Lord *present* to yourselves. We enter into the mindful present of Christ as we enter into the deepest part of our selves.

Re-presenting Christ

I began this book by stressing the importance of the Trinitarian perspective for understanding any aspect of Christian prayer. From this point of view the prayer advocated by a teacher such as Teresa differs from the Buddhist meditation techniques that we discussed in Chapter 1. As this element is so central to the Christian understanding of mindfulness, I would like to give the rest of this chapter over to a discussion of how Teresa and John treat this central theme in Christian contemplation. For Teresa, this 'looking' at Christ is the *sine qua non* for true Christian prayer. In fact, she says in the passages quoted above that if we are unable to make special meditations or contemplations on Christ, we should just 'look at him': 'I am not asking you now to think of Him, or to form numerous conceptions of Him, or to make long and subtle meditations with your understanding. I am asking you only to look at Him. For who can prevent you from turning the eyes of your soul (just for a moment, if you can do no more) upon this Lord?' (CV: 26.3). 'Behold', she continues, 'He is only waiting for us to look at Him, as He says to the Bride.[11] If you want Him you will find Him. He longs so much for us to look at Him once more that it will not be for lack of effort on His part if we fail to do so.'

Having introduced us to the importance of mindfulness, the rest of her *Way* ends up being a mindful reflection on the nature of this relationship with Christ by using the prayer that he gave his disciples: the Lord's Prayer. Indeed, we could say her preoccupation is how we can place our minds in the present tense of Christ: this will be achieved for her by our mindful contemplation of the Lord's Prayer. As she says at the beginning of her commentary on the Lord's Prayer:

'Our Father, which art in the Heavens.' O my Lord, how You reveal Yourself as the Father of such a Son, and how Your Son reveals Himself as the Son of such a Father! May You be blessed for ever and ever. Should not so great a favour as this, Lord, to have come at the end of the prayer? Here, at the very beginning, You fill our hands and grant us so great a favour that it would be a very great blessing if our understanding could be filled with it so that the will would be occupied and we should be unable to say another word. Oh, how appropriate, daughters, would perfect contemplation be here! Oh, how right would the soul be to enter within itself, so as to be the better able to rise above itself, that this holy Son might show it the nature of the place where He says His Father dwells – namely, the Heavens! (CV: 27.1)

By simply stating the words 'Our Father, which art in heaven' the mind is immediately placed into the presence/present of Christ which, of course, is in Trinitarian relationship with the Divine Father. This becoming present to oneself (in oneself and beyond oneself as she states here) is thus not only the beginning of contemplative mindfulness but also its fruit and its end; as she says, 'should this not have come at the end?'

Such a Trinitarian mindful contemplation of the nature of our souls in Christ will thus reveal to us a favourite theme of Teresa's – the heavens that lie within our souls, to be grasped by means of contemplative prayer. For as she states at the beginning of chapter 28: 'I assure you that for minds which wander it is of great importance not only to have a right belief about this but to try to learn it by experience, for it is one of the best ways of concentrating the mind (*and thoughts*) and recollecting the soul' (CV: 28.1/CE: 46.1). For Teresa this insight – that our souls will find rest in the mindful presence of God – is not just fundamental for our understanding of the mindful way but, as she emphasizes throughout her writing, it will be a cause of great delight and pleasure for us:

> You know that God is everywhere; and *this is a great truth, for*, of course, wherever the king is, or so they say, the court is too: that is to say, wherever God is, there is Heaven. No doubt you can believe that, in any place where His Majesty is, there is fullness of glory. Remember how Saint Augustine tells us about his seeking God in many places and eventually finding Him within himself. Do you suppose it is of little importance that a soul which is often distracted should come to understand this truth and to find that, in order to speak to its Eternal Father and to take its delight in Him (*para regalarse*

con El), it has no need to go to Heaven or to speak in a loud voice? However quietly we speak, He is so near that He will hear us: we need no wings to go in search of Him but have only to find a place where we can be alone and look upon Him present within us. Nor need we feel strange in the presence of so kind a Guest; we must talk to Him very humbly, as we should to our father. (CV: 28.2/CE: 46.2)

In this masterful paragraph Teresa combines the mindful notion of being present to Christ in silent prayer with the tradition of *recogimiento* we discussed in Chapter 3. Her mindful prayer truly becomes a prayer of the heart at this point – the heart wherein we find Christ within. Thus she describes her mindful way a few paragraphs later as the ability of being able to form the habit of 'looking at nothing and staying in no place which will distract these outward senses', for by following such a practice a person 'may be sure that they are walking on an excellent road, and will come without fail to drink of the water of the fountain, for they will journey a long way in a short time. They are like one who travels in a ship, and, if he has a little good wind, reaches the end of his voyage in a few days, while those who go by land take longer' (CV: 28.5).

And, of course, as has been stressed throughout her discourse, by embarking upon such a mindful way, embedded within ordinary practices – the 'pots and pans' of our everyday lives – we shall begin to notice the outer effects of this new practice of mindful recollection:

> These souls have already, as we may say, put out to sea; though they have not sailed quite out of sight of land, they do what they can to get away from it, in the time at their disposal, by recollecting their senses. If their recollection is genuine, the fact becomes very evident, for it produces certain effects which I do not know how to explain but which anyone will recognize who has experience of them. It is as if the soul were rising from play, for it sees that worldly things

> are nothing but toys; so in due course it rises above them, like a person entering a strong castle, in order that it may have nothing more to fear from its enemies. It withdraws the senses from all outward things and spurns them so completely that, without its understanding how, its eyes close and it cannot see them and the soul's spiritual sight becomes clear.
> (CV: 28.6)

This will of course become Teresa's famous description of the soul as the 'Interior Castle' that we mentioned in the previous chapter and that will form the basis of her late commentary on the soul, *The Interior Castle/Las Moradas*, which would be her last published work (see Tyler 2013, chapter 6).[12] For now she stresses how the effects of mindful prayer will change our perceptions and relationship with the world around us as we become caught up in this vital work:

> But if we cultivate the habit [of recollection], make the necessary effort and practise the exercises for several days, the benefits will reveal themselves, and when we begin to pray we shall realize that the bees are coming to the hive and entering it to make the honey, and all without any effort of ours. For it is the Lord's will that, in return for the time which their efforts have cost them, the soul and the will should be given this power over the senses. They will only have to make a sign to show that they wish to enter into recollection and the senses will obey and allow themselves to be recollected.
> (CV: 28.7)

Not for everyone

Much of Teresa's preoccupation in *The Way* is to show how mindfulness (*oración mental*) can be integrated into a spiritual seeker's life. However, as I have stressed throughout this chapter, there are certain aspects of Teresa's programme that would distinguish it from the types of contemporary mindfulness we explored earlier in the book. First, there is the importance of entering into relationship with the Transcendent Other – Christ – and the importance she gives to this as the source and goal of prayer. For her true prayer begins in Christ and ends in us. There are two consequences of this approach with which I would like to conclude this chapter. The first is that for Teresa mindfulness or *oración mental* is not for everyone. At the end of chapter 30 she gives a striking account of an old nun she knew who wasn't able to grasp the practices she has called *oración mental* (in CE she actually says she couldn't grasp 'prayer'). However, the nun was still able to achieve what Teresa calls 'perfect contemplation' by means of the recitation of short prayers such as the Lord's Prayer:

> I know a person who could never practise anything but vocal prayer but who kept to this and found she had everything else; yet if she omitted saying her prayers her mind wandered so much that she could not endure it. May we all practise such mindfulness as that. She would say a number of Our Fathers, corresponding to the number of times Our Lord shed His blood, and on nothing more than these and a few other prayers she would spend several hours. She came to me once in great distress, saying that she did not know how to practise mindfulness,[13] and that she could not contemplate but could only say vocal prayers. *She was quite an old woman and had lived an extremely good and religious life.* I asked her what prayers she said, and *from her reply* I saw that, though keeping to the Lord's Prayer, she was experiencing pure contemplation, and the Lord was raising her to be with Him in union. She spent her life so well, too, that her actions made it clear she was receiving great favours. So I praised the Lord and envied her her vocal prayer. (CV: 30.7/CE: 52.4)

As Teresa stresses throughout her writings, and in particular in *The Way of Perfection*, the way of prayer is unique for each person. We must not try and force our prayer and contemplation into a particular box or form. If our prayer-time becomes obsessed with the question 'Am I doing this correctly?', then something has gone terribly wrong. For her, as we have seen, we should not force our thoughts into corners and ways that are uptight. In contrast to some of the paths we explored at the beginning of this book, Teresa would not say mindfulness/mental prayer is for everyone. Rather, it is for those who find it helpful in establishing a relationship with the one she says loves us. She is urging us to find, above all else, *spiritual freedom* and this can only be found by relaxing, in her eyes, into the arms of the one who loves us – Jesus Christ.

Which brings me to the second mark that clearly distinguishes her way from that of contemporary practitioners of mindfulness – the importance she places on the mindful relationship with Christ. Accordingly, I want to end this chapter by saying a few words about how this relationship is developed in mindful contemplation and the role that visualization, ikons and pictures will play in developing this aspect of Christian mindfulness. As she puts it: 'You will find it very helpful if you can get an image or a picture of this Lord – one that you like – not to wear round your neck and never look at but to use regularly whenever you talk to Him, and He will tell you what to say. If words do not fail you when you talk to people *on earth*, why should they do so when you talk to God?' (CV: 26.9). As St Paul says in the letter to the Philippians, Jesus Christ is the image or ikon of the invisible God and this notion of Christ as the window into the mystery of the Trinity is one that is developed by both Teresa and her co-worker, St John of the Cross, with whose reflections I shall conclude this chapter.

The use of pictures

Although St Paul had stated that Jesus Christ was the 'image' or 'ikon' of the unseen God, Christianity, like Judaism and Islam, has always had an uneasy relationship with the notion of picturing God. Had not the Second Commandment given to Moses expressively forbidden the making of images of God? This is an injunction held to this day within both Judaism and Islam. Throughout its 2,000-year-long history, Christianity has held an uneasy truce with the making and veneration of images. As well as some of the most beautiful artefacts and images of the divine created by its artists it has also at times periodically swung into periods of iconoclasm – destruction of all images as perverse or dangerous. John and Teresa were writing during the midst of one of these periods of iconoclasm, and while Teresa wrote *The Way* this process was getting under way around Europe. A couple of decades later when her co-worker, St John of the Cross, came to write his commentaries on his poetry, known today as the *Ascent of Mount Carmel* and the *Dark Night of the Soul*, the reformed attack on religious art was in full spate and so it was with some caution he turned to the subject that Teresa had introduced in *The Way*.

In his 1986 commentary on St John, the Swiss theologian Hans Urs von Balthasar suggests that the saint was in fact fighting on two fronts: 'against the Reformation's depreciation of all religious images, of all church ornament' and 'against the development of a more passionate style of art in the Renaissance and early Baroque'; in contrast to both, von Balthasar suggests that John 'advocates a rather medieval view of religious art' (1986, p. 154) – that is, a 'middle way' between the iconoclastic desire to destroy all representations of God and the baroque indulgence of all sensual forms of representation. As with Teresa's mindful middle way between materialism and transcendentalism, John too offers sage and considered advice as to how we incorporate imagery into our prayer. For when John considers the Christian life in the *Ascent of Mount Carmel* he sees two desires interacting in the soul. First there is the 'habitual desire to imitate Christ in all deeds, bringing your life into conformity with His' (A: 1.13.3).[14] This is the 'imitation of Christ' that derives ultimately from his study of St Thomas Aquinas and the importance he places on the forming of habit in our relationship with Christ. But second, there is what can be called the 'mystical turn' and the desire to 'approach God the more closely the more (the person) withdraws from all imaginative forms, images and figures' (A: 3.13.1). This latter, which is normally referred to as the apophatic way or *via negativa* (as opposed to the cataphatic way or *via positiva* of the first approach) is the one that is normally associated with St John of the Cross because of his association with the phrase 'dark night of the soul'. Yet it would be a mistake, I would argue, to see his theology and approach to contemplation entirely dictated by this latter. In fact, he is often at pains to stress the need for both approaches if we are to have a healthy relationship with the Divine.

Thus, when beginning his discussion of the use of images and pictures as an aid to meditation John begins from the latter, apophatic, position, as he pokes fun at those who resort to excessive use of such images to populate their prayer lives:

> Hence, to begin our discussion on the subject of oratories, some individuals never grow tired of adding images of one kind or another to their oratories, or of taking delight in the arrangement and adornment of these images so the place of prayer will appear well decorated and attractive. But they do not love God more when it is arranged in this way instead of that, rather they love him less, since the delight they find in these ornate paintings withdraws their attention from the living person represented. (A: 3.38.2)

The danger, of course, is that the images can be seized upon by the hungry ego as a substitute for the unknowing centre of love that is God. For, he suggests, 'people extinguish the spirit by wanting to conduct themselves in a way different from the way God is leading them'. Therefore, with regard to artworks we should consequently 'pay heed not to the feelings of delight or sweetness, not to the images, but to the feelings of love that are caused' by these images (A: 3.13.6). We recall St Peter on beholding the transfigured Lord on Mount Tabor wanting 'to make three tents' for Elijah, Christ and Moses rather than entering into the 'dazzling darkness' of the cloud that covers them (Luke 9.33).

When our souls are touched by the incomprehensible and inexpressible love of God our first natural human reaction is to pin it down, make it tame, and somehow safe. John's counsels are continually warning us against any attempt to tame the unruly and wild Holy Spirit of God. The ultimate goal, then, of these uses of images is:

> To direct the spirit to God in this kind of good, we should keep in mind that for beginners it is permissible and even fitting to find some sensible gratification and satisfaction in the use of images, oratories, and other visible objects of devotion. With this delight they are assisted in renouncing worldly things from whose taste they are not yet weaned or detached. This is what we do with a child when we desire to take something away from it; we give it another thing to play with so it will not begin to cry when left empty-handed. (A: 3.39.1)

Yes, we respect the power of images to help form our consciousness in mindful prayer, yet we also remember that they are means to an end, for they will lead to the goal we are seeking – the formless apprehension of the Divine:

> But in order to advance, the spiritual seeker should strip herself of all these sweetnesses and appetites in which the will takes pleasure, for the pure spirit is bound to none of these objects but turns only to interior recollection and mindful

intercourse with God (*recogimiento interior y trato mental con Dios*). Although they derive profit from images and oratories, this is very transitory, for their spirit is immediately elevated to God in forgetfulness of all sensory objects.[15]

John's *trato mental con Dios* is his elegant combination of Teresa's descriptions of *oración mental* and prayer as a *trato* with God. What we are striving for, stresses John, is towards a *trato mental* with God – literally a mindful communion. Accordingly, to foster this communion John suggests that in seeking a place to meditate, seekers:

> Should not look for a spot pleasant and delightful to the senses, as some usually do, lest they become absorbed in the recreation, gratification, and delight of the senses rather than in God in spiritual recollection. A solitary and austere location is beneficial for the sure and direct ascent of the spirit to God without the impediment or detainment caused by visible things. (A: 3.39.2)

John describes three types of place we might consider for practising our daily meditation. First there are the peaceful places where we naturally find we can move into the contemplative space. These places, he says, 'have pleasant variations in the arrangement of the land and trees and provide solitary quietude, all of which naturally awakens devotion' (A: 3.42.1). Yet, as stressed above, these attractive places will become in themselves a hindrance if we glory in the beauty and peace of the place rather than seeing them as a means to an end – that is, access to the *trato mental* with God. We may indeed become too comfortable in our prayer places. Having always acquired spiritual sweetnesses or insights in one place we may become accustomed to only meditating there. This again for John can be harmful. Our regular prayer and meditation can lapse into a habitual and possibly unthinking process whereby we lose the savour that must lie at the heart of the encounter with the Divine: 'if seekers strive for recreation of their appetites and sensory satisfaction, they will rather find spiritual dryness and distraction; for spiritual satisfaction and contentment are found only in interior recollection'.[16]

The second type of place we may choose for our meditations are spots at home or far away where we have previously encountered spiritual insights and delights. Again, we must be careful to separate the 'naked encounter' with the Divine in unknowing with the pleasures and comforts associated with a particular spot. As he states with great psychological acuity:

> [God] grants his favor so the heart of the recipient will have a natural inclination toward that place, and will sometimes experience intense desires and longings to return there. But on returning, that person discovers that the place is not what it was before because these favors do not lie within one's own power. God bestows these graces when and how and where he wills without being bound to place or time or to the free will of the recipient. (A: 3.42.3)

Again, as with Teresa's account of prayer, John is wanting to stress that the engine and dynamo of prayer lies with the Other – that is, God – rather than ourselves. We can do all we can to dispose ourselves, but it is the Other who will show us the ways to the Heart.

The final place we may choose for our meditation are those spots that are associated with a particularly intense religious practice or religious ceremonies. John mentions the holy places of the Bible such as Mount Sinai and Mount Horeb, but we could add the other great pilgrimage places of the world – such as Jerusalem, Rome, Varanasi or Mecca – to which pilgrims still flock today. However, as before, spiritual gifts are given from the generosity of God rather than controlled by the efforts of our ego. We may make the long (and expensive) pilgrimage to India or the Holy Land and ultimately find that the spiritual insight we longed for comes unexpectedly, perhaps in a railway waiting room or while out shopping. We can make our plans and pursue the Divine through these earthly manifestations, but ultimately it will be up to God to decide when and how the Divine moment of insight will arrive. That, for Christians, is not in our gift, only God can decide this: 'God alone knows why he chooses one place in which to receive praise more than another. What we should know is that he does all for our own benefit and so he may hear our prayers in these places – or anywhere we beseech him with integral faith' (A: 3.42.6).

God finds us where we are, and so uses the loving-kindness of memory to stir our souls to love of God even long after the event has occurred:

> Only for the sake of moving the spirit to love should the soul at times recall the images and apprehensions that produced love. The effect produced by the remembrance of this communication is not as strong as the effect at the time the communication was received, yet when the communication is recalled there is a renewal of love and an elevation of the mind to God. This is especially true when the soul remembers some figures, images, or supernatural feelings. These are usually so imprinted on it that they last a long time; some are never erased from the soul. These apprehensions produce, almost as often as remembered, divine effects of love, sweetness, light, and so on – sometimes in a greater degree, sometimes in a lesser – because God impressed them for this reason. This is consequently a great grace, for those on whom God bestows it possess within themselves a mine of blessings. (A: 3.13.6)

Thus, in summary, we find in John's counsel a 'middle-way' between a type of prayer and meditation that seeks absolute removal of all mental objects and sources of devotion, and another that would cling unnecessarily to an image, picture, or even a place, meditation cushion or meditation time! Prayer and meditation, for John, have a natural ebb and flow – we must be constantly striving, he urges, to free ourselves from the stickiness of the ego that is constantly trying to restrict the flow of Divine in our prayer relationship. As Teresa had warned, we must not get ourselves uptight in prayer or 'stuck in a corner'. For John, like Teresa, 'spiritual freedom' lies at the heart of his wise counsel to the spiritual seeker.

Summary

I have argued in the last two chapters that we can see in the writings of the sixteenth-century Spanish spiritual masters a 'school of mindfulness'. I have argued that their notion of *oración mental* is a forerunner in many ways to what we would today call mindfulness.

The fullest description of this 'mindful path' is perhaps in St Teresa's 'Way of Perfection' which, as we have unpacked it here, can be seen as a mindful way to spiritual freedom by means of humility, detachment and concentration on the love of the other. However, in detailing Teresa's mindful way in this chapter I have also emphasized where her teaching differs from the Buddhist and contemporary teachings on mindfulness that we encountered at the beginning of this book. In particular, I have emphasized two aspects of that *différance*: first there is Teresa's (and John's) emphasis on the relationship with the Divine Other. It is inconceivable to imagine a type of prayer for these two seekers that does not put this 'mindful communion' at its heart. In this respect their prayer is probably better described as heartfulness than mindfulness. Yet, in visualizing the Divine Other, both guides – especially John – present a subtle 'middle-way' in describing this relationship. As well as covering the use of images, ikons and pictures in our meditations and prayer, this 'middle-way' even extends to the type, frequency and position of our prayer. As with so much else, both spiritual masters recognize the subtle power of the ego to subvert the Divine pull on the soul, leading even prayer to become another block between us and the 'spiritual freedom' that constitutes our 'mindful communion' with the Divine.

The second essential difference between Teresa and John's mindful path and some contemporary practices of mindfulness arises from this first one. That is, for Teresa and John, mindfulness, or contemplative prayer, is not in itself essential for the 'mindful communion' with the Divine. As in the case of the old nun we heard Teresa describing earlier, there are those who will be 'frightened by the very word "mindfulness"' and for such people, she declares, it is important that they are not forced into types of prayer that do not suit them.[17] Mindfulness may be necessary for the spiritual seeker in the Christian tradition, but it is never prescriptive or essential. Both Teresa and John never fail to recognize this.

Finally, it is important to stress that both Teresa and John recognize the necessity for the 'horizontal axis' in prayer and our need to relate prayer to those around us. If prayer becomes an end in itself then something has gone badly awry. As she forcibly puts it in her last work, the *Interior Castle*:

> When I see people very diligently trying to discover what kind of prayer they are experiencing and so completely wrapt up in their prayers that they seem afraid to stir, or to indulge in a moment's thought, lest they should lose the slightest degree of the tenderness and devotion which they have been feeling, I realize how little they understand of the road to the attainment of union. They think that the whole thing consists in this. No, sisters, no; what the Lord desires is works. If you see a sick woman to whom you can give some help, never be affected by the fear that your devotion will suffer, but take pity on her: if she is in pain, you should feel pain too; if necessary, fast so that she may have your food, not so much for her sake as because you know it to be your Lord's will. That is true union with His will. (*The Interior Castle* 5.3.11)

At the end of the day, she reminds us, God only asks two things of us: 'love for His Majesty and love for our neighbour' (*The Interior Castle* 5.3.8). As we recall, Teresa stressed that for success on the mindful path we need three aspects: humility, detachment and love of neighbour. And it is to this latter that we will turn in Chapter 5 as we examine the life and teachings of Thomas Merton – the twentieth-century master of mindfulness.

Exercise Four: Prayer of the Name

As Teresa indicates, you will have probably noticed that undertaking the stillness exercises we have described so far often leads to a confusion of thoughts swarming the mind – Teresa's 'wild horses' that drag the mind away from meditation. Frequently when leading these sessions people will say to me: 'I wish I could pray more but the moment I sit down to pray I have lots of distracting thoughts which stop me going further.' When I hear this I often think it's a bit like saying: 'I've always wanted to see a football match but when I went to the local stadium last week I was very disappointed – the grass was covered by all these men running around in bright-coloured clothes chasing after a ball – if they hadn't been there I would have seen a good football match!' Working with the thoughts – 'the distractions' – *is* prayer. Which is not to underestimate the task before us; the mind, as the Buddha said, is a wild elephant in rut, so we will need to work carefully with the thoughts to lead to the peace we are seeking in contemplation. Fortunately, generations of pray-ers and seekers have left plenty of tips and guides to this and it is to this task we turn now in this next series of exercises.

o O o

As before, compose the time and place in which to perform the exercise, taking some time to do some of the body and breathing exercises already described. Now become aware of your thoughts. Don't follow them, just observe them. Notice what is troubling or bothering you, exciting or depressing you. The trick is not to get caught up in the thoughts but to observe them arising, gaining strength and then passing away.

Now take a simple word or phrase and simply repeat it. Traditional religious practice is to take a name of God such as 'Jesus', 'My Lord', 'Saviour', etc. and repeat it. The repetition can be silent or out loud. Try both in different prayer sessions to see the effects. When choosing the phrase to be repeated, it is good not to give it much thought but instead to go with the first phrase that comes to your heart. In addition, as we suggested in the previous exercise, the repetition of the phrase can be made on each in-breath as we observe the movements of breathing as we did previously. Continue the repetition for ten minutes as before. At the conclusion notice what has been difficult, what pleasant, and which thoughts that arose caused the most difficulty.

o O o

Of all the exercises encountered in this book this is one of the most ancient and widespread among the religions of the world. The Christian Orthodox tradition refers to it as the 'Jesus Prayer' and from early Christian times it has been recommended highly as a means to finding peace in prayer. Here is an ancient description:

> Abba Evagrius said, 'I was tormented by the thoughts and passions of the body, so I went to find Abba Macarius. I said to him, "Father, give me a word to live by." Abba Macarius said to me, "Secure the anchor rope to the rock and by the grace of God the ship will ride the devilish waves of this beguiling sea." I said to him, "What is the boat? What is the rope? What is the rock?" Abba Macarius said to me, "The ship is your heart; keep guard over it. The rope is your mind, secure it to our Lord Jesus Christ, who is the rock who has power over all the waves ... Because it is not difficult, is it, to say with each breath, 'Our Lord Jesus, have mercy on me: I bless thee, my Lord Jesus, help me.'"' (Pseudo-Macarius, *Coptic Cycle of Sayings*, in Clément 2013, pp. 204–5)

The image of the repetition of Jesus' name as the rope taking us down into the unconscious depths is a beautiful one, and precisely describes the effects of this powerful prayer. As we practised it above, the prayer in this tradition is done both vocally out loud as well as silently 'in the heart' – I have even seen it done by monks as they work in the fields! In the Islamic tradition it is known as the *dhikr*, the remembrance of the names of God, and is usually performed in a group setting to powerful effect. Hindus and Buddhists recommend the repetition of the 'mantra' and contemporary groups such as the World Community for Christian Meditation recommend the use of a simple phrase such as 'Maranatha'. Whichever method we adopt, all these groups have found that the repetition of a sacred phrase can be a powerful means of moving in prayer from the head to the heart. From the perspective of the discussion of this chapter it is a powerful prayer that combines the 'apophatic' and 'cataphatic' elements we analysed earlier.

Variations on the Exercise

As will probably be apparent by now, this versatile exercise may be performed on many levels. We can simply let the imagination stay with the repeated phrase as it counters the other thoughts in our minds, or we can say it out loud, alone or in a group. The latter can be accompanied by musical instruments or singing – again a strong tradition in the Islamic Sufi tradition. Western Christianity adopted the Eastern practice of repeating the phrase while counting beads – the 'rosary' – which repeats the phrases of prayers such as the 'Hail Mary' while counting the beads. Many of these traditional prayers are in fact pilgrim prayers and are well adapted to the rhythm of walking. Again, try either repeating a simple phrase or using a traditional prayer while walking slowly and mindfully. They can have a wonderful effect in calming the mind and moving us to the place of the heart. Finally, if the repetition of a phrase is not helping us we can always follow Teresa and John and concentrate in prayer on a picture, ikon, image – or even a flower or natural landscape. All are possible means of bringing the troubled mind to the 'harbours of salvation'.

Notes

1 Avila, July 2017.

2 '*Pienso poner algunos remedios para tentaciones de relisiosas y el intento que tuve de procurer esta casa, digo que fuese con la perfeción que se lleva – dejado el ser de nuestra mesma Constitución – y lo que*

más el Señor me diere a entender, como fuere entendiendo y acordándoseme, que como no sé lo que será, no puedo decirlo con concierto; y creo es lo mijor no le llevar, pues es cosa tan desconcertada hacer yo esto. El Señor ponga en todo lo que hiciere sus manos para que vaya conforme a su santa voluntad, pues son éstos mis deseos siempre, aunque las obras tan faltas como yo soy.'

3 Throughout this chapter I have used two Spanish editions of Teresa's text called in English *The Way of Perfection* – the so-called Valladolid and Escorial versions – as found in Efrén de la Madre de Dios and Steggink's version in the *Biblioteca de Autores Cristianos* edition (with occasional reference to the Toledo version). I have used as the basis of my English translation that found in Allison Peers's translation. Allison Peers (and Kavanaugh and Rodriguez) largely concentrate on the Valladolid version introducing variants in the Escorial codex as they arise. Where, as in the above quote, I have relied on the Escorial version I have indicated it with CE – using CV for the Valladolid codex. In passages where my interpretation differs more markedly from Allison Peers's, I have supplied the original Spanish. In passages of CV translation where I have added extracts from CE I have marked this by placing them in italics. For full bibliographical details see the Bibliography. See Tyler 2013, chapter 1, for more on the methodology behind my approach.

4 '*La una es amor unas con otras; otra, desasimiento de todo lo criado; la otra, verdadera humilidad, que aunque la digo a la postre, es la principal y las abraza todas.*' Although she places humility last, she states that it is the most important quality and embraces the other two.

5 http://www.cabinetmagazine.org/issues/2/western.php   'From Western Marxism to Western Buddhism.'

6 The last words in italics are in CE but not CV.

7 '*Hay unas almas y entendimientos tan desbaratados como unos caballos desbocados, que no hay quien las haga parar. Ya van aquí, ya van allí, siempre con desasosiego.*'

8 '*Todos los que pudieren ir por él llevarán descanso y seguridad; porque, atado el entendimiento, vase con descanso.*'

9 '*¡Oh almas, que no podéis tener mucho discurso de entendimiento, ni podéis tener el pensamiento, sin mucho divertiros, en Dios!, ¡acostumbraos, acostumbraos! Mirad que sé yo que podéis hacer esto, porque pasé muchos años por este trabajo de no poder sosegar el pensamiento en una cosa – y eslo muy grande –, mas sé que no nos deja el Señor tan desiertos, que si llegamos con humildad no nos acompañe; y si en un año no pudiéremos salir con ello, sea en más. Digo que esto, que lo puede: acostumbrarse a andar cabe este verdadero Maestro*' (CE: 42.2). This is a difficult passage to translate and one with variant mean-

ings both in CE and CV – compare Allison Peers's and Kavanaugh and Rodriguez's differing translations at this point.

10 'Representad al mismo Señor junto con vos y mirad con qué amor y humildad os está enseñando. Y creedme, mientras pudiereis no estéis sin tan buen amigo. Si os acostumbráis a traerle cabe vos y El ve que lo hacéis con amor y que andáis procurando contentarle, no le podréis -como dicen- echar de vos; no os faltará para siempre; ayudaros ha en todos vuestros trabajos; tenerle heis en todas partes: ¿pensáis que es poco un tal amigo al lado?'

11 Reference to Song of Songs 2.14, 16 and 5.2.

12 As she puts it in CV: 28.9: 'And now let us imagine that we have within us a palace of priceless worth, built entirely of gold and precious stones – a palace, in short, fit for so great a Lord. Imagine that it is partly your doing that this palace should be what it is – and this is really true, for there is no building so beautiful as a soul that is pure and full of virtues, and, the greater these virtues are, the more brilliantly do the stones shine. Imagine that within the palace dwells this great King, Who has vouchsafed to become your Father, and Who is seated upon a throne of supreme price – namely, your heart.'

13 CE has 'did not know how to pray' here.

14 I am using here the Spanish version found in *San Juan de La Cruz: Obras Completas* (Biblioteca de Autores Cristianos 2002) and the English translation of Kavanaugh and Rodriguez in *The Collected Works of St John of the Cross* (ICS 1979). Where I have made my own translation I have stated it. *The Ascent of Mount Carmel* is abbreviated with A, and *The Dark Night of the Soul* with DN. Full bibliographical references are to be found in the Bibliography. As before, where my own translation differs I have given the Spanish in full.

15 'Pero para ir adelante también se ha de desnudar el espiritual de todos esos gustos y apetitos en que la voluntad puede gozarse; porque el puro espíritu muy poco se ata a nada de esos objetos, sino sólo en recogimiento interior y trato mental con Dios; que, aunque se aprovecha de las imágenes y oratorios, es muy de paso, y luego para su espíritu en Dios, olvidado de todo lo sensible.'

16 'Porque, si procuran recrear el apetito y sacar jugo sensitivo, antes hallarán sequedad de espíritu y distracción espiritual; porque la satisfacción y jugo espiritual no se halla sino en el recogimiento interior.'

17 See CV: 24.1: 'As a matter of fact, there are a great many people who seem terrified at the very name of contemplation or mindfulness.' ('Que hay muchas personas en hecho de verdad que sólo el nombre de oración mental o contemplación parece las atemoriza.')

5

Thomas Merton – Mindful Clarity of Heart

Spring Moon

Spring moon greets evening star.
Pearl light in the West,
March's evening glow.
Migrating cranes
Bring promise of joy.
Perhaps tomorrow
Will bring the thaw.[1]

'Portrait of the monk as a young tear-away'

At the beginning of his best-selling autobiography *The Seven Storey Mountain* (Merton 1948), Thomas Merton, twentieth-century mystic, political activist, writer and Cistercian monk, wrote:

> On the last day of January 1915, under the sign of the Water Bearer, in a year of great war, and down in the shadow of some French mountains on the borders of Spain, I came into the world. Free by nature, in the image of God, I was nevertheless the prisoner of my own violence and my own selfishness, in the image of the world into which I was born. (Merton 1948, p. 3)

This passage, written barely four years after entering the Cistercian ('Trappist') Abbey of Our Lady of Gethsemani in

Kentucky, is classic early Merton – dramatic, incisive and raising more questions than it answers. The facts of his birth were that he was born during a snowstorm on 31 January 1915 in Prades, a French Pyrenean village near the border with France. His parents, the American Ruth Jenkins and New Zealander Owen Merton, were both artists and had met as students in Paris. In Forest's words they had 'an artist's attraction to southern light, inexpensive living and the presence of friends nearby' (Forest 1991, p. 5). Merton acknowledged in his autobiography the artistic debt he owed to his parents, especially his father, and this artistic skill and insight would be something that would inform his later work especially in writing and photography: 'His vision of the world was sane, full of balance, full of veneration for structure, for the relations of masses and for all the circumstances that impress an individual identity on each created thing' (Merton 1948, p. 3).[2] This ability to see what the Jesuit poet Gerard Manley Hopkins (himself influenced by St Bonaventure) called the *in-stress* of objects – what the medievals termed the *quiddity* of created objects – was a significant element of Merton's spirituality and can be seen most clearly in his striking later photography.

With the advance of World War One the Mertons left France and returned to New York. Here, in 1921 when Merton was six years old, his mother Ruth was diagnosed with stomach cancer. She decided to communicate this to young Thomas by writing him a letter. Merton's account of reading this letter 'under the maple tree in the back yard' evokes a poignant mixture of sorrow and spiritual yearning:

> I worked over [the letter] until I had made it all out, and had gathered what it really meant. And a tremendous weight of sadness and depression settled on me. It was not the grief of a child, with pangs of sorrow and many tears. It had something of the heavy perplexity and gloom of adult grief, and was therefore all the more of a burden because it was, to that extent, unnatural. (Merton 1948, p. 14)

Again, the Merton tone is there – portentous but perplexed – and we can sense some of the confusion the little boy felt, but also the power he found in the words that he sat with and 'made out'. Words were to remain his lifelong friends and allies in all his future battles.

After five more years in the United States, Owen Merton decided it was time for the family (minus Thomas's younger brother John Paul) to return to France, and this they duly did in 1925 when they returned to St Antonin near Toulouse. As with so much of Merton's life, artistic impressions and sensibilities had a strong impact on him and he described the 'clean, ancient stone cloisters, those low and mightily rounded arches hewn and set in place by monks' of the monasteries of southern France that made a strong impression on him at this time. Yet here, at St Antonin, Owen was diagnosed with tuberculosis while Thomas spent time at the Lycée at Montauban, France. This was followed by a period when Thomas was sent to school in England – first at Ripley Court School and then at Oakham in Rutland. Thomas described England in his autobiography as the land where 'every impact of experience seemed to reach the soul through seven or eight layers of insulation' (Merton 1948, p. 61), and so it was to be as he lived with his Aunt Maud in Ealing, West London, 'where all the Victorian standards stood entrenched in row upon row of identical houses'. Thomas's combination of being from an artistic background and being fluent in French 'added up to practically everything that Mrs Pearce [the headmistress of Ripley Court] and her friends suspected and disliked' (Merton 1948, p. 64). While on holiday in Scotland and preparing to enter Oakham School, Thomas again received a message from his remaining parent which heralded further disease and death. This time his father, taken ill in London, wrote a mysterious telegram: 'Entering New York Harbour. All well'. Later, Thomas wrote of this time: 'I sat there in the dark, unhappy room unable to think ... without a home, without a family, without a country, without a father, apparently without any friends, without any interior peace or confidence or light or understanding of my own – without God, too, without God, without heaven, without grace, without anything' (1948, pp. 71–2). This existential nihilism accompanied Thomas throughout his father's decline and death from a brain tumour in 1931 and his move from Oakham to Cambridge in 1933 where he studied Modern Languages at Clare College. According to his autobiography, his own nihilism combined with the 'dark, sinister atmosphere of Cambridge' to produce lethal consequences. Reflecting on these events 20 years later, he felt there was 'a subtle poison in Europe ... some kind of a moral fungus, the spores of which floated in that damp air, in that foggy and half-lighted darkness' (Merton 1948, p. 126). For the young Thomas Merton 'most of the people were already morally dead, asphyxiated by the stream of their own strong, yellow tea or by the smell of their own pubs and breweries, or by the fungus on the walls of Oxford and Cambridge'. Although his superiors asked him to omit detailed reference to these events in his autobiography his subsequent biographers (see Furlong 1985 and Forest 1991) mention two events in particular: first, that Merton got a girl 'not of our class' pregnant; the girl and child apparently later died during the Blitz although this was never verified. The second traumatic event seems to have been a sort of drunken mock crucifixion performed on Merton at a party that got out of control and necessitated calling the Cambridge police. Merton apparently retained a scar on one of his palms for the rest of his life and sometimes referred to it jokingly as 'my stigmata'.

Merton left Europe in 1934, the continent of his birth, never to return. Towards the end of his life he did express a strong desire to visit Wales, but England, it seems, never held such a great attraction for him ever again (see Allchin 2006).

The call to silence

Back in the United States, the 'poison' of England seemed to have been drawn out of him and he began to flourish as a writer, journalist and student at Columbia University. As well as his studies in Spanish, German, Law, Geology and Contemporary Civilization, he worked on the student magazines *The Jester*, *The Columbia Review* and *The Spectator*. This work and the contacts he made would profoundly influence his future writing career for, among others, he met here Robert Giroux who would later publish *The Seven Storey Mountain*. From this time onwards his reading and interest was directed more and more to Christianity, and in particular medieval Christianity. Important influences at this time included Étienne Gilson's *The Spirit of Medieval Philosophy* and William Blake, concerning whose poems he wrote his Masters thesis in 1938–9. Blake's combination of religious mysticism and practical critique of the 'dark satanic mills' of the nascent Imperialist Empire appealed in particular to Merton who himself at this time flirted with socialism and communism as ways out of the inequality and despair he saw in the Depression-era society around him. 'What a thing', he wrote, 'to live in contact with the genius and holiness of William Blake that year … By the time the summer was over I was to become conscious of the fact that the only way to live was to live in a world that was charged with the presence and reality of God' (Merton 1948, p. 189). Again, through providence or luck, he found such a world 'charged with the grandeur of God' in the writings of the nineteenth-century Jesuit poet Gerard Manley Hopkins, as interpreted by G. F. Leahy's biography of the poet. On a September night in 1939 in his lodgings on West 114 Street as Europe slid into war, Merton read about Hopkins's conversion to Roman Catholicism while he was a student at Oxford in 1866 and wrote: 'All of a sudden, something began to stir within me, something began to push me, to prompt me. It was a movement that spoke like a voice: "What are you waiting for?" it said. "Why are you sitting here? Why do you still hesitate? You know what you ought to do? Why don't you do it?"' (Merton 1948, p. 215). After a while he could contain himself no longer – he put on his coat and walked the nine blocks to the Roman Catholic church of Corpus Christi where he had been attending mass. He was welcomed by the priest and in the parlour finally stated: 'Father, I want to become a Catholic.'

From this moment onwards Merton seemed swept up in the tide of the Holy Spirit that would eventually deposit him at the Cistercian Monastery of Our Lady of Gethsemani in Kentucky. However, before arriving at Gethsemani Merton tried his vocation with the Franciscans in New York who accepted him for the novitiate in June 1940. However, after reflecting upon his application over the summer he felt that he had not been sufficiently honest with the Franciscans and had omitted certain details of his past life – such as having fathered a child in England. Once the fathers heard this they felt it was best that Merton withdraw his application and reconsider his vocation. Finally in 1941, having taught for a year at a Franciscan college, he decided to spend Holy Week 1941 on retreat at Gethsemani. As he entered the doorway to Gethsemani, with its inscription *Pax Intrantibus – Peace to All who Enter*, on a still April evening with the Easter moon in the sky, Merton was overwhelmed by 'the effect of that big, moonlit court, the heavy stone building with all those dark and silent windows': a moonlit place he would later so wonderfully describe in the 'Fire Watch' of his *Sign of Jonas* (Merton 1953). 'This', he wrote, 'is the center of America. I had wondered what was holding the country together, what has been keeping the universe from cracking in pieces and falling apart' (quoted in Forest 1991, p. 73).

Following the narrative of *The Seven Storey Mountain*, written some four years after the event, Merton's entrance into the novitiate of Gethsemani in February 1942 marked the end of Merton's 'life in the world' and the beginning of the rest of his life in the quiet and peace of the Abbey. The book itself had been written in 1946 with the encouragement of the Abbot,

Dom Frederic, the son of a bookbinder and publisher, but with a certain misgiving by Merton himself. His old friend Robert Giroux, now at the publisher Harcourt and Brace, accepted the manuscript for publication. It was an immediate runaway success and sold 600,000 copies in cloth-back alone and many more in paperback. Merton seemed to have struck a chord with a war-weary world that was seeking a way back to its spiritual roots. By turning his face against modern Western culture Merton had ironically offered an alternative vision of salvation for that culture. As Forest puts it, '*The Seven Storey Mountain* was an electrifying challenge to the idea that human happiness consists mainly of a proper diet, a good job, a comfortable address and an active sex life' (Forest 1991, p. 90). Yet with the benefit of hindsight he would later describe his autobiography, whose success often seemed to embarrass him, as the work of a 'young man' whose certainties and clear assertions, especially regarding other Christian denominations (Protestantism and Anglicanism come off particularly badly in the *Mountain*) and other faiths (although a meeting with a Hindu *swami* in New York before he joined the Order seemed to have made a big impact on him, as had the life and teachings of Mahatma Gandhi) he later repudiated.

Merton and mindfulness

From the perspective of the present book this transformation of Merton from the traditionalist Trappist monk to one of the first twentieth-century Christian writers to seriously embrace dialogue with Eastern religions, especially Buddhism and Hinduism, is instructive. If we are attempting to find a *rapprochement* between Buddhist mindfulness and Christian contemplation, by way of the contemporary practice of mindfulness, then a study of Merton will help reveal the way forward with this dialogue. To this end we can begin by asking ourselves: what brought about this change and how could the somewhat conventional and rather prudish monk of the 1940s transform into the open-minded and pioneering 'campaigning monk' of the 1960s?

No doubt the answer to some of this lay in Merton's personality itself. Like John of the Cross, Merton seemed to possess a similar spiritual and artistic insight into 'awareness' – perhaps given to him by his artistic parents, especially his father. In a more dramatic fashion he recounts in his spiritual journals a famous account of an 'epiphany' he had on 18 March 1958 while in the nearby town of Louisville on an errand:

> In Louisville, at the corner of Fourth and Walnut, in the center of the shopping district, I was suddenly overwhelmed with the realization that I loved all those people, that they were mine and I theirs, that we could not be alien to one another even though we were total strangers. It was like waking from a dream of separateness, of spurious self-isolation in a special world, the world of renunciation and supposed holiness. The whole illusion of a separate holy existence is a dream. (Merton 1966, p. 140)

From this point onwards Merton would not be concerned with cultivating a spurious elite 'religiosity' but with concentrating on awareness of 'God in all things' by cultivation of the 'authentic self' through spiritual freedom (see Tyler 2000). It is no accident that this new insight coincided with a renewed interest in psychoanalysis which he had earlier rejected in *The Seven Storey Mountain* as dangerous to religious belief.

From hereon he became increasingly interested in the social and political movements of the United States in the 1950s and 1960s, especially the Catholic Worker Movement, the anti-nuclear movement and the struggle for black rights – famously being silenced for his anti-war writings at this time. His *Peace in the Post-Christian Era* was not published until long after his death, in 2004, and reading it today it seems as fresh a critique of contemporary military adventures as it did then.

From the perspective of the present book the most important fruit of this late 1950s epiphany was a reversal of his earlier views on non-Catholic Christians and people of other faiths. In 1960 he wrote to the newly elected Pope John XXIII, who was about to initiate the Second Vatican Council, informing him of his latest retreats held for Protestant ministers. The Pope's Secretary wrote back to say how interested he was in this development and encouraged Merton's work. In 1965, having long asked permission, Merton was finally granted his wish to live as a hermit in the grounds of Gethsemani. His life now took on a new intensity as all its various and disparate elements seemed to come together. He wrote in his journals of his passionate communion with the beautiful Kentucky landscape around him while continuing his campaigning on social issues and his exploration of 'inner' space through psychoanalysis and studies in other religious contemplative approaches, especially Sufism, Hasidism and Buddhism.

Accordingly, for the remainder of this chapter I would like to concentrate on Merton's later engagement with Buddhism and his development of mindful attention – in particular, through what we would call contemplation of the heart. However, like for Teresa, for Merton authentic contemplation could most certainly not be developed in isolation from the concerns and worries of the wider humanity in the midst of whom we live. Accordingly, having looked at Merton's understanding of contemplation I shall move to a discussion of how he relates this to our place in the created order, and the implications for our relations with our fellow human beings, before some final words on Merton's mindful 'clarity of the heart'.

Contemplation

Shortly after completing his best-selling *Seven Storey Mountain*, Merton began a new book that would distil his thoughts on contemplation at the time: *Seeds of Contemplation* (1949).

Like Teresa of Avila's *Way of Perfection*, this book was intended for the wider public, written from the perspective of one who had retreated from society so as to perfect the art of contemplation. Yet, Merton being Merton, he could not leave this text alone and over the next two decades, as his own views towards Christian life changed, he tinkered with the text (Grayston in a perceptive study has identified five versions – see Grayston 1985). The result of this process was the publication of *New Seeds of Contemplation*, published in 1961. Yet this was not to be his last word on the subject: his *Climate of Monastic Prayer*, published posthumously in 1969 and thereafter reprinted as *Contemplative Prayer* (1973), reveals how far the restless soul had travelled, especially during the important years of the 1960s and his engagement with Zen Buddhism. In the account that follows I shall draw primarily on these texts, supplementing them with his writings on Zen and engagement with other faiths.

In a letter to his Sufi correspondent, Abdul Aziz, of 2 January 1966, Merton wrote: 'Strictly speaking I have a very simple way of prayer. It is centered entirely on attention to the presence of God and to His will and His love. That is to say that it is centered on faith by which alone we can know the presence of God ... My prayer is then a kind of praise rising up out of the center of Nothing and Silence' (Merton 1985, p. 62).

For Merton contemplation – or to use the word of his French contemporary Simone Weil, 'awareness' – was at the heart of the spiritual life. This was not just something for 'religious professionals' but something that was gifted to all as their divine right. His whole life can be seen as an attempt at living with and trying to articulate the strange processes of the 'subtle nothingness of prayer'. The comments to Aziz on the nature of contemplative prayer are reflected in a passage from *Contemplative Prayer*:

> We should not look for a 'method' or 'system', but cultivate an 'attitude', an 'outlook': faith, openness, attention, reverence,

expectation, supplication, trust, joy. All these finally permeate our being with love in so far as our living faith tells us we are in the presence of God, that we live in Christ, that in the Spirit of God we 'see' God our Father without 'seeing'. We know him in 'unknowing'. (Merton 1973, p. 39)

Prayer and contemplation are not, then, an 'add-on' to life for Merton, they are at the heart of life. This 'divine unknowing', what the medievals called the *stulta sapientia* (literally 'foolish wisdom', cf. 1 Corinthians 1), is the beginning of all wisdom and the heart of Christian contemplation. 'It is the seriousness', Merton reminds us, 'of breathing when you're drowning' (Baker and Henry 1999, p. 154).

Influenced by his study of the desert fathers and mothers, the young Merton stressed the subtle delusions we can be led into by our prayer practice. While a seeker can 'give up the pleasures and ambitions of the world' (Merton 1949, p. 125) they can easily be replaced by 'a higher and more subtle' spiritual ambition. Like his mentor St John of the Cross, Merton had an innate suspicion of the self-deception that can be caused by spiritual highs or seraphic enthusiasms leading us to become attached to 'the good things of their little enclosed world' (Merton 1949, p. 126). His later denunciation of seeking a 'system' or 'method' in prayer was something he had developed long ago, influenced, as I have said, by his love of St John of the Cross:

> Sometimes contemplatives think that the whole end and essence of their life is to be found in recollection and interior peace and the sense of the presence of God. They become attached to these things. But recollection is as much a creature as an automobile. The sense of interior peace is no less created than a bottle of wine. The experimental 'awareness' of the presence of God is just as truly a created thing as a glass of beer. (Merton 1949, p. 126)

This subtle self-delusion (so long ago identified by the desert elders) extends both ways, of course, as Merton perceptively recognized. On the one hand, there is the attachment to spiritual 'goods'; on the other, there is an attachment to outer schemes, activities and 'getting things done' – what he calls, quoting Cassian, a 'dragon's gall': 'Blinded by their desire for ceaseless motion, for a constant sense of achievement, famished with a crude hunger for results, for visible and tangible success, they work themselves into a state in which they cannot believe that they are pleasing God unless they are busy with a dozen jobs at the same time' (Merton 1949, p. 127). Such de-centred activism, he believed, would lead to what we would today call 'burn-out': 'then they wake up and discover that their carelessness has involved them in some gross and obvious sin against justice, for instance, or against the obligation of their state. And so they drown' (Merton 1949, p. 128).

Importantly from the point of view of the argument of the present book, as well as this external detachment Merton stresses the need for what he calls an 'interior detachment' (Merton 1949, p. 129). As with our discussion of Teresa and *oración mental*, Merton stresses that the role of prayer and contemplation is to get 'beneath' our thoughts to what he calls at this stage 'the heart'. Interestingly, in the light of our discussion in previous chapters, the type of prayer he wants us to overcome is what he terms 'mental prayer' – literally a concentration on and development of mental images in prayer. Prayer, for him, is not about getting some 'interesting ideas' about God – or ourselves for that matter (Merton 1949, p. 136). For the real purpose of meditation (as he calls it at this stage) is to teach us how to 'shake ourselves free of created things and temporal concerns' (Merton 1949, p. 137). This is the 'unknowing knowing' he would later speak about in *Contemplative Prayer*. Once the mind has been thwarted in meditation, insight begins:

> Do you think your meditation has failed? On the contrary: this bafflement, *this darkness and anguish of helpless desire is the true fulfillment of meditation* ... when it gets beyond the level of your understanding and your imagination it is really bringing you close to God, for it introduces you into darkness where you can no longer think of Him. (Merton 1949, p. 138, Merton's italics)

Thus, to find interior peace and recollection we must, he suggests, become detached from the *desire* for interior peace and recollection: 'you will never be able to pray perfectly until you are detached from the pleasures of prayer' (Merton 1949, p. 129).

In retrospect, this early fascination with the 'knowing unknowing' at the heart of contemplation would make Merton perfectly receptive to the ways and approaches of Zen that he would come to appreciate so much later on his development.

Beginning with an extended correspondence and conversations with the noted Zen master D. T. Suzuki (see Merton 1985), Merton became completely absorbed in the study of Zen, leading to one of his last completed works, a collection of essays: *Zen and the Birds of Appetite* (Merton 1968b). Zen-practice, the awareness of Zen-mind and the practice of *satori* developed the insights that Merton had originally had in *Seeds of Contemplation* so that by the time he edited the final version of *New Seeds of Contemplation* in 1961 he could incorporate these insights with lengthy revisions and the addition of several new chapters that melded his earlier Christocentric observations on prayer with his later insights from Zen.

The Zen master

'Who said Zen?', wrote Merton in his journal for 1965 – 'wash out your mouth if you said Zen. If you see a meditation going by, shoot it.' Even at this late stage of his engagement with

Buddhism his critical sense never departed him and he was as aware as ever of the subtle self-deceiving 'orientalism' that often overtakes Western study of Eastern literature. Against the backdrop of the 1960s psychedelic revolution, his comments are refreshingly critical:

> In an age where there is much talk about 'being yourself' I reserve to myself the right to forget about being myself, since in any case there is very little chance of my being anybody else. Rather it seems to me that, when one is too intent on 'being himself', he runs the risk of impersonating a shadow ...
> This is not a hermitage – it is a house. ('Who was that hermitage I seen you with last night?')
> What I wear is pants.
> What I do is live.
> How I pray is breathe.
> Who said 'Love'? Love is in the movies.
> The spiritual life is something that people worry about when they are so busy with something else they think they ought to be spiritual. Spiritual life is guilt. (Merton 1998 – May 1965)

Had Merton himself succumbed to these temptations as a young man? If so, it would explain his vehement exposure of their deceptions in middle age. For as much as he critiques the search for 'real spirituality', he also questions the search for the 'real self' that somehow lies beneath the surface of our 'everyday self'. For him: 'Buddhist meditation, but above all that of Zen, seeks not to *explain* but to *pay attention*, to *become aware*, to *be mindful,* in other words to develop a certain *kind of consciousness that is above and beyond deception* by verbal formulas – or by emotional excitement' (Merton 1968b, p. 38, Merton's italics). Zen therefore encourages a certain type of 'authentic metaphysical intuition which is also existential and empirical' (Merton 1968b, p. 38), for the Zen practitioner sees 'what is right there and does not add any comment, any interpretation, any judgement, any conclusion' (Merton 1968b, p. 53). Thus Zen provided a means for Merton whereby he could articulate 'a breakthrough, an explosive liberation from one-dimensional conformism, a recovery of unity which is not the suppression of opposites but a simplicity beyond opposites' (Merton 1968b, p. 140). This was a breakthrough, or revolution, not just for the practitioner but for the whole of a culture dominated by the dead-ends of objectification and reification: 'The inner self is as secret as God and, like Him, it evades every concept that tries to seize hold of it with full possession. It is a life that cannot be held and studied as object, because it is not a "thing"' (Merton 2003, p. 7).

Merton's embrace of Zen and his integration of it into his Christian practice is clearly shown in the two new opening chapters added to the 1961 revision of *New Seeds of Contemplation*, which also reflects the new mission he felt for his writings in the 1960s. The earlier book, he says in his 1961 preface, had been written 'in a kind of isolation'; however, this later book will now be written for all, to address 'the loneliness of people outside any monastery ... outside the Church' (Merton 1961, p. 9). And to achieve this aim he introduces the new mindful language of Zen into his old accounts of Christian contemplation. He now describes contemplation, adapting the phrases of his beloved Zen, as: 'The highest expression of our intellectual and spiritual life. It is that life itself, fully awake, fully active, fully aware that it is alive. It is spiritual wonder. It is spontaneous awe at the sacredness of life, of being' (Merton 1961, p. 13). All Merton's favourite tropes are here: like the Buddha, we are quite literally 'awakened' from our sleep by contemplation. Mindful awareness is our destiny as human beings and, as with the philosophers, awe and wonder are the seeds from which this new form of contemplation grows. Once placed in its axis, we appreciate not only the wonder of our being but of all being – the 'sacredness of life'. Yet, in a deft move, Merton in these opening paragraphs attaches his Zen wonder to the Christian source of being – God – reflecting those early passages from Étienne Gilson that had been so instrumental in his conversion all those years ago. For the sense of wonder, unlike that of a Zen context, leads us to appreciate 'the fact that life and being in us proceed from an invisible, transcendent and infinitely abundant source'. For contemplation is 'awareness of the reality of that source. It knows the source, obscurely, inexplicably, but with a certitude that goes beyond reason and beyond simple faith' (Merton 1961, p. 13). This is a move no Buddhist could surely make but it is deftly and subtly introduced by Merton. In many respects this passage is typical of the style of later Merton where he splices Zen, Christian contemplation, psychological insight and his own personal experience into each other to produce an apparently seamless narrative belying its complexity. The apparent simplicity of his prose is testament to his skill as a wordsmith.

The mindful eye

There is also now in his writings a new-found appreciation of that which goes 'beyond words'. Merton had inherited his parents' eye for artistic insight but in these later years he now takes quite literally the need for the symbolic as we move 'beyond all knowing and "unknowing"' (Merton 1961, p. 13). This is nowhere better illustrated than by his late flowering love of photography and image. As he writes in September 1964, his love of the camera begins to meld with his 'Zen-like' appreciation of the odd and the unusual: 'After dinner I was distracted by the dream camera, and instead of seriously reading the Zen anthology I got from Louisville Library, kept seeing curious things to shoot, especially a mad window in the old tool room of the woodshed ... The whole place is full of fantastic and strange subjects – a mine of Zen photography' (Merton 1998, 24.9.64). And even more ecstatically two days later: 'Camera back. Love affair with camera. Darling camera, so glad to have you back! Monarch! xxx' (Merton 1998, 26.9.64).

The fruits of this Zen-centred love of photography are in the remarkable portfolio of late photographs shot by the monk. What is also striking in the pictures is Merton's love of wasteplaces, weeds and neglected nooks and crannies. Here again we see echoes of that other important early influence on the 'myriad-minded monk' who had been so instrumental in his conversion to Catholicism: Gerald Manley Hopkins. Merton's 'Zen-like shapes' have a family resemblance to Hopkins's 'in-scapes' which themselves owe much to his reading of medieval attitudes to 'quiddity' – 'this-ness'. When we examine Merton's journals there is more than a passing resemblance to those of Hopkins. Both record the minutiae of weather, atmosphere, humidity and temperature. Indeed, Merton's journal entries in 1965 rarely omit a reference to the weather, our mindful attention to being leading, as he suggests, to a mindful attention to the whole cosmos around us:

> Fierce cold all night, certainly down to zero and inside the house almost freezing, though embers still glowed under the ashes in the fireplace. (Merton 1998, 31.1.65)

> The cold weather finally let up a bit today – the first time in about a week that it had been above freezing. Zero nights, or ten above. Very cold, sometimes even cold in bed. (Merton 1998, 4.2.65)

> At midnight I woke up, and there was a great noise of wind and storm. Rain was rolling over the roof of the hermitage heavy as a freight train. The porch was covered with water and there was a lot of lightning. Now at dawn the sky is clean and all is cold again (yesterday warm). (Merton 1998, 27.11.65)

Like the Jesuit, he 'sees God in all things' and his awareness of weather, temperature and climate blends into his wider ecological and environmental awareness. The journals contain many beautiful descriptions of the forests and landscape around the hermitage and monastery and it is clear that Merton responded to them on a fundamentally deep level of mindfulness.

Like Hopkins, Merton also loves what the English poet calls 'the wet and the wildness':

> What would the world be, once bereft
> Of wet and of wildness? Let them be left,
> O let them be left, the wildness and wet;
> Long live the weeds and the wilderness yet.
> (*Inversaid*, Hopkins 1985, p. 51)

What von Balthasar writes of Hopkins could equally be applied to Merton's journals: 'In the creative sources of natural things, whether they be enduring or completely transitory, like water and clouds and the light and the shade of landscape, the novice, the scholastic framed himself in this encounter with the Creator of all nature' (von Balthasar 1969, p. 53).

Merton's beloved desert fathers and mothers had spoken of the 'book of creation', and in his new-found liberty of the hermitage Merton enjoys this encounter with the secret author of all things in the smallest and most delicate aspects of his creation – whether that be a caterpillar, mist, snow, frost or the tiny titmice that sing around his hermitage. For the late Merton, mindful appreciation of art is as important as Zen-like sitting for us to achieve the awareness of being that he stressed at the beginning of *New Seeds*. In *Disputed Questions*, also published in 1961 (Merton 1961a), he states that the goal of art is to enhance contemplation – a 'way of seeing' the world as well as developing a *habitus* within the artist: an ability to see stability, order and integration in the created world. For now: 'There is no longer any place for the kind of idealistic philosophy that removes all reality into the celestial realms and makes temporal existence meaningless ... we need to find ultimate sense here and now in the ordinary humble tasks and human problems of every day' (Merton 1968b).

This awareness of the present moment – 'the power of now' – leads to a wider cosmic awareness and our own place within creation. Faced with the ecological disasters of the late twentieth century, we are forced more and more to reassess our place within creation and our commitments and responsibilities to the world around us. Merton in the 1960s talked about the need to address those problems 'which threaten our very survival as a species on earth' (Merton 1968b, p. 30) and in this he was prescient in his negative response to the new agricultural technologies being introduced at the Abbey of Gethsemani by his fellow monks: heavy agricultural machinery, invasive pesticides and the removal of the old horses. When such concerns became mainstream in 1962 with the publication of Rachel Carson's *Silent Spring*, he responded positively to her critique: 'We are in the world and part of it and we are destroying everything because we are destroying ourselves, spiritually, morally and in every way. It is all part of the same sickness' (Merton 1996, p. 274).

Merton saw the late twentieth-century destruction of the environment as a counterpoint to self-hatred and self-destruction, and only when we respect ourselves will we be able to respect the created order. In this his argument reflects that of Pope Francis in his encyclical *Laudato si'* (Pope Francis 2015). Throughout Merton's journals we hear about his love of the environment around him and the need to respect this: 'We must not try to prepare the millennium by immolating our living earth, by careless and stupid exploitation for short-term commercial, military or technological ends which will be paid for by irreparable loss in living species and natural resources' (Merton 1994, p. 75).

This new embodied spirituality took on a very personal aspect for Merton when in his early fifties he fell in love with a nurse at the local hospital when he was admitted for treatment in 1965. As we have seen, as a young man he vacillated between indulgence of the body and repression of his desires. After years of struggle with late middle age he began to integrate the two so that when he fell in love again as an older man he was able to act with restraint and discernment while still being able to appreciate the gift that had gratuitously been given him:

> The ambiguity that love has brought ... is no cause for disturbance. Somehow in the depths of my being I know that love for her can coexist with my solitude, but everything depends on my fidelity to my vocation that there is no use trying too much to rationalize. It is *there*. It is a root fact of my existence. I cannot pretend to understand it perfectly. (Notebooks of 1966, quoted in Tyler 2000, p. 83)

For him this new dimension of his life became as much a journey of 'unknowing and faith' as his contemplative exercises. He had not just entered a school of the head but a school of the heart that gave as much importance to the arts, liturgy and embodied experience as it did to scholastic theology. As he put it in *Zen and the Birds of Appetite*:

> In our need for whole and integral experience of our own self on all its levels, bodily as well as imaginative, emotional, intellectual, spiritual, there is no place for the cultivation of one part of human consciousness, one aspect of human experience, at the expense of others, even on the pretext that what is cultivated is sacred and all the rest profane. A false and divisive 'sacredness' or 'supernaturalism' can only cripple us. (Merton 1968b, p. 30)

For the late Merton, therefore, contemplative practice was to become compatible with 'every other form of intuition and experience – whether in art, in philosophy, in theology, in liturgy or in ordinary levels of love and of belief' (Merton 1961, p. 14). It would engender what he calls in one of his last writings the birth of the 'new man', so much needed by humanity and the cosmos at this critical time: 'It is a birth which gives a definite meaning to life. The first birth, of the body, is a preparation for the second birth, the spiritual awakening of mind and heart ... It is a deep spiritual consciousness which takes man beyond the level of his individual ego' (Preface to the Japanese edition of 'The New Man' in Merton 1981, p. 146). Such a re-birth will embrace all the aspects of being: philosophical, theological, aesthetic and libidinal, so that they '"die" to be born again on a higher level of life' (Merton 1961, p. 14). Only by these means, he suggests, can we preserve our humanity in these difficult times: 'the direct and pure experience of reality in its ultimate root is man's deepest need'. Therefore 'contemplation must be possible if man is to remain human' (Merton 1981, p. 95). Merton's intuition here is, I feel, reflected in the current resurgence of the mindfulness movement, for as much as anything it is a search to restore humanity in a dehumanizing and commodified world dominated by global technocrats, big business and the military establishment – all targets, at one time or another, of Merton's waspish invective.

Therefore, for Merton, contemplation and mindfulness are a 'sudden gift of awareness' that leads to 'an awakening to the real within all that is real' (Merton 1961, p. 14) and such an awakening *must*, for him, lead us to have a social conscience.

An engaged social conscience

Earlier in the book we essayed the problem of the promotion of a type of mindfulness that places individual experiences of bliss at the expense of a wider social conscience. As we have seen, Merton would later see contemplation as something that could not be divorced from the struggles and sufferings of our times. The twentieth century through which he lived saw the most horrendous atrocities committed. Merton lived through them all and wanted his readers, especially those now engaged in contemplative practices, to reflect especially on their complicity with unequal and ultimately murderous social structures. When he arrived at Columbia University in the 1930s he was conducted through a tour of the city morgues as part of his 'contemporary civilization' course. The sight of the corpses of so many poor and homeless people made him realize the privileged life he had been leading and the need for greater social justice even in the wealthy and developed city of New York.

By instilling in us a deeper sense of reality and being, contemplation will also, he argues, plant within us a deeper appreciation of the part we each play in the maintenance of violent and unjust structures. In *Faith and Violence* he places Western consumerist behaviour in the context of a radical social analysis that still bites today:

> The population of the affluent world is nourished on a steady diet of brutal mythology and hallucination, kept at a constant pitch of high tension by a life that is intrinsically violent in that it forces a large part of the population to submit to an existence which is humanly intolerable ... The problem of violence, then, is not the problem of a few rioters and rebels, but the problem of a whole structure which is outwardly ordered and respectable, and inwardly ridden by psychopathic obsessions and delusions. (Merton 1968a, p. 78)

We are systemically part of the structures of violence that envelop our society and we have complicity in the violence of society. As Merton makes clear in the first lines of the *Seven Storey Mountain* quoted at the beginning of this chapter, we are born into those violent structures and one of the key elements of our spiritual development is to understand how we are to respond to these violent structures in a contemplative fashion.

Merton's social ethic also brilliantly combines the need for social engagement to be rooted in deep contemplation and awareness of self. In the famous 'Letter to an Activist' written to Jim Forest on 21 February 1965, Merton emphasizes the importance of not attaching to results of the activism: 'face the fact that your work will be apparently worthless and even achieve no result at all, if not perhaps results opposite to what you expect' (Merton 1985). 'All the good that you will do', he adds, 'will come not from you but from the fact that you have allowed yourself, in the obedience of faith, to be used by God's love.' Along with alcohol, sex, food and consumer goods, it seems we can add social activism to the list of things we use to fill the void that lies at the centre of our aching hearts. 'The great thing', he concludes, 'is to live, not to pour out your life in the service of a myth: and we turn the best things into myths.' Good social action can be as much part of the 'dragon's gall' that blinds us to the truth as any destructive action. We must become aware, he counsels, of the subtle poison of the ego entering even into this apparently innocuous part of our lives too. He had, he said, a 'deep unresolved suspicion of activism and activistic optimism in which there seems to me to be a very notable amount of illusion (though no one speaks intelligently *against* it) because I find in it no rest, no certainty, no real deep sense' (Merton 1998, 26.5.64).

Mindful clarity of heart

For the final decade of his life at Gethsemani, Merton taught the monks in formation at the abbey as their novice master. As part of this role he had to give regular talks on aspects of monastic and Christian contemplative life. These lectures are preserved for us today in two forms – original tapes of the selected lectures held by the Thomas Merton Foundation and the recently published lecture notes that Merton made for these same lectures (ed. O'Connell in Merton 2005). In them we find Merton working on the final synthesis of all the influences that had directed his path to the divine: the Christian contemplative tradition, Zen Buddhism, Hasidism, Sufism, psychology and social awareness. Examination of these lectures reveals Merton offering his own gloss on the ancient tradition of Western monasticism – adapting it to the needs of the modern era while preserving continuity with the old ways. As he wrote in a famous letter to the French theologian Jean LeClerq, he saw contemporary monasticism as having a simple choice – either it must busy itself with its own survival or break out 'into deep waters' and pursue the prophetic role it had inherited from the desert fathers and mothers (Merton 2008).

An interesting example of this, and pertinent to the theme of this book, is how he expounds Cassian's writings on prayer in Book Nine of his *Conferences* – the same text we explored in Chapter 2, and also familiar to St Teresa of Avila.[3] He begins the lecture with his own translation of Book 9:3.2: 'For whatever our soul was thinking about before the time of prayer inevitably occurs to us when we pray as a result of the operation of memory. Hence we must prepare ourselves before the time of prayer to be the prayerful persons that we wish to be.'[4] Having presented the passage to the novices Merton asks them: 'How should you want to be at the time of prayer?' before picking on one Br Cuthbert (clearly a pious type) with the question: 'How would you like to be found at the time of prayer, Br Cuthbert?' The good brother responds (as if replying by rote): 'A peace resulting from docility to the will of God'. Without missing a beat Merton takes the response in his stride and proceeds to present his own interpretation of Cassian, informed, as I argue here, by his Zen readings. For, Merton stresses, what we should seek in the pursuit of prayer and contemplation is 'a kind of peace where we have clarity – this is the word we should emphasize – there should be clarity in prayer'. He continues:

> We should strive for clarity. Our prayers should be intelligent. What is stressed are good intentions. Yes good intentions are OK. But we need intelligent good intentions ... Therefore in prayer it is important that we seek the truth with intelligence ... If in prayer you are trying to sharpen up a scientifically perfect concept of God or something you're going to have a hard time. Most of the time it isn't possible at all. But if you

can get clarity about your relationship with God, which is certainly possible, that is what you are looking for in prayer.

From the point of view of our investigation, what is fascinating is that Merton introduces the concept of 'clarity' into Cassian's reflections on prayer – a notion that is not in Cassian's passages themselves. Commenting on Cassian in *Zen and the Birds of Appetite*, Merton would later say how he finds Cassian's emphasis on *puritas cordis*/purity of heart 'not yet Zen because it still maintains that the supreme consciousness resides in a distinct heart which is pure ... and ready to receive a vision of God. It is still very aware of a "pure", distinct and separate self-consciousness' (Merton 1968b, p. 9). In his talks with the novices, even before *Zen and the Birds of Appetite* was written, Merton was clearly already unhappy with Cassian's concept of purity of heart and has replaced it with the more Zen-like 'clarity'.[5] As he continues in the lectures:

> You need to learn to pray without the help of your imagination and emotions which you would like very much to help you ... When you are here that goes ... when that goes we drop the idea of prayer ... One of the most important things in the life of prayer is to let a great deal go on without knowing quite what is going on. Without messing with it. Without interfering with it.

This notion of prayer seems to me to come very close to the understandings of mindfulness we essayed earlier in the book. Yet, as with Cassian and Teresa, for Merton the aim of this mindfulness is not mindfulness for mindfulness sake, but rather to create the conditions for a loving relationship with the Triune Lord. As he continues:

> This accounts for long periods in your spiritual life which are called periods of dryness – in which you want to pray and you want to read but you don't seem to be getting much out

of anything but you keep on doing it anyway – and you don't see any results and you sometimes wonder if it's worth any trouble and you go and ask somebody advice about it and you don't get any help because you can't be helped ... If you could be helped it wouldn't be worth it ... God alone helps you ... you have to have a faith and trust in this.

Being a mid-Western American, however, his analogy of this 'breakthrough moment' is somewhat unlike that of John Cassian and Teresa of Avila. As he continues: 'Then suddenly you come out in a whole new place. It's what they call a breakthrough ... Like the three bells of the fruit-machine ... it is the *kairos* of the spiritual life.'

This *kairos* of Christian prayer is for Merton both an encounter with the Divine as well as – and here he draws on his Zen studies – a 'breakthough into a deeper level of yourself'. What is also striking in Merton's account is that the existence of the horizontal and vertical axes of prayer that we saw in Cassian and Teresa are re-emphasized and deepened. Just as Cassian warns us of using prayer or meditation for our own ends (bodily, mental or spiritual) and Teresa had insisted that all true Christian prayer leads to 'Good works! Good works! Good works!', so Merton emphasizes that Christian prayer, the breakthrough to the deeper level of self, is there to enable the situation whereby we break out into the world of delusion and help our fellow humanity (as evidenced in his own controversial work with peace-workers, anti-nuclear campaigners and black rights activists in the 1960s). Such a realigned relationship to the world is such for Merton that it should even question religious institutions themselves when they get in the way of this reforming zeal:

> A great deal of religious life prefers you to be a useful functioning unit. Run your parish and don't get involved in this deep interior life stuff – it means trouble! That's the sort of trouble the monastic life is meant to foment! ... A deeper

level of experience that society does not really encourage and does not really want.

Merton himself of course famously had his writings suppressed because of such attitudes, yet perhaps, as Generation Text takes up the anti-establishment bases of mindfulness, Merton's own Zen-Christianity, with its scepticism of authority based on loving devotion of the Lord, may have come of age. Such insight is, he had written in *New Seeds*, 'an awakening, enlightenment and the amazing intuitive grasp by which love gains certitude of God's nature and dynamic intervention in our daily life' (Merton 1961, p. 15) which will not lead to sharpening 'ideas about God' (least of all 'scientific ideas about God'), but rather it is the *kairos* invitation to participate in God's freedom, presence and action in the world. This is what he calls the '*point vierge*', 'the virginal knowledge' – the clarity of mindful insight – enabling us once again to participate in the 'cosmic dance' of creation:

> When we are alone on a starlit night; when by chance we see the migrating birds in autumn descending on a grove of junipers to rest and eat; when we see children in a moment when they are really children; when we know love in our own hearts; or when, like the Japanese poet Bashô we hear an old frog land in a quiet pond with a solitary splash – at such times the awakening, the turning inside out of all values, the 'newness', the emptiness and the purity of vision that make themselves evident, provide a glimpse of the cosmic dance. (Merton 1961, p. 192)

The final dance

Merton's interest in Eastern religions reached its climax with his fateful visit to Asia in 1968. He had been invited to address the Bangkok Conference of Asian Benedictine and Trappist

Superiors, and in October he set off for Calcutta via Bangkok. Following a conference there he travelled to Dharamsala to meet the newly exiled Fourteenth Dalai Lama and his Tibetan community in exile. The Dalai Lama would later call him 'a close friend or brother' (Mitchell and Wiseman 1999, p. 260) and the two established a deep and natural rapport. From Northern India, Merton moved to Sri Lanka in late November and there occurred, some two weeks before he died, a moment of profound mindful clarity such as he had described in his writings. While viewing the famous statues of the reclining Buddha at Polonnaruwa: 'I was suddenly, almost forcibly, jerked clean out of the habitual, half-tied vision of things, and an inner cleanness, clarity as if exploding from the rocks themselves, became evident, obvious ... All problems are resolved and everything is clear, simply because what matters is clear' (Merton 1974, pp. 233–4).

Sadly, having delivered his paper on 'Marxism and Monastic Perspectives' to the Abbots' conference in Bangkok on 9 December 1968, Merton was found dead later that afternoon in his accommodation. It seems as though after a shower a faulty fan had fallen on him and electrocuted him. Ironically, his body was flown back to the States in a USAF airplane in the company of the bodies of the US military fighting in Vietnam, for whom he had so tirelessly campaigned. He was buried at Gethsemani. After his morning conference on the day he died, a nun had complained that he had said nothing about conversion. Accordingly, his final recorded words were: 'What we are asked to do at present is not so much to speak of Christ as to let him live in us so that people may find him by feeling how he lives in us' (quoted in Forest 1991, p. 216).

Exercise Five: One-pointed Heart Devotion

If you have a heart, you can be saved. (Abba Pambo)

In *Contemplative Prayer* Merton stressed the heart-centre of Christian contemplation. As he wrote there: 'In the "prayer of the heart" we seek first of all the deepest ground of our identity in God. We do not reason about dogmas of faith, or "the mysteries". We seek rather to gain a direct existential grasp, a personal experience of the deepest truths of life and faith, *finding ourselves in God's truth*' (Merton 1973, p. 85).

In this exercise we will follow the path of devotion as we focus on the heart of the Divine.

As before, we take time to settle ourselves into the exercise. After the composition of place and time, simple body awareness and the repetition of the sacred phrase to still the mind, we now turn our attention to the heart area. Concentrate on the heart and feel the touch of God's love in the heart. If the heart feels cold or prickly, imagine Christ gently touching it and warming it. Likewise, if there is a part of your body or memory that hurts, allow the touch of Christ to enter it, gently and firmly. Stay with the touch of God. If you feel moved to it, have a conversation with your Divine Master and allow God to speak directly into your imagination. Conclude with a short prayer of thanksgiving.

Variations on the Exercise

At this point in our journey we have moved from knowledge to love of God – this in the Christian tradition centres on the Heart of Christ. By performing this exercise we begin the process of intimately sharing with the nature of Christ through his Sacred Heart. This is also a good point to introduce Scripture into our exercises. This can be done in various ways. The traditional Benedictine method – known as 'divine reading'/ *lectio divina* – is where we take a passage of Scripture and then savour it. In the context of these prayer exercises we might want to take a passage such as the one we used in Exercise Three and read it slowly and carefully before we do our prayer, either aloud or silently (this works well in a group too):

> When it was evening on that day, the first day of the week, and the doors of the house ... were locked for fear ... Jesus came and stood among them and said, 'Peace be with you ... as the Father has sent me, so I send you.' When he had said this, he breathed on them and said to them, 'Receive the Holy Spirit ...' (John 20.19-22)

We then repeat this process two or three times. This is not biblical study or exegesis. Rather, we are putting the sweet words in our mouths and allowing the flavours to come out. After the usual stillness exercises we then just allow phrases or sentences to stay with us: 'the doors of the house were locked', 'Peace be with you', 'Receive the Holy Spirit', etc.

Another way of using Scripture in prayer is referred to as the Ignatian method after the life and teachings of St Ignatius of Loyola. Here again we take time to place ourselves in the presence of the Divine having read the passage slowly and carefully a few times. In contrast to the Benedictine method we now imagine ourselves in the house with the disciples locked up in fear. We imagine the faces of the people around us – the colour of their eyes, their clothes, the expressions on their faces. Are they old or young? What are they talking about? What is their fear? What is my fear? How do I feel in this situation? What can I hear outside the door? Now I imagine Jesus among us. Look at his face – what is he wearing? What colour is his hair? His eyes? Now hear his words 'Peace be with you'. Notice the tone of his voice, the reaction of those around him. Now hear the rest of his words: 'As the Father has sent me, so I send you'. How do I feel about that? What is the reaction of others in the room? Now he begins the process of breathing on those around him. Watch him breathe on the people one by one. Hear his words 'Receive the Holy Spirit'. Notice the effect it has on each person as he breathes on them. Finally he comes round to you. How do you feel about this encounter? Are you anxious, excited, worried? Look into Jesus' face as he comes to you – does he smile, is he serious? Now hear his words 'Receive the Holy Spirit' and feel his breath as he breathes on you.

St Ignatius suggests that we end such a prayer session with a short conversation, or colloquy as he calls it, with God. So end with a conversation with Christ. Talk to him about how it was for you and what has happened to you. Also, be aware of what you understand him to be asking you to do.

Finally, Ignatius recommends a short prayer of thanksgiving and a formal prayer such as the Lord's Prayer to finish with.

Notes

1 Salisbury, March 2000.
2 The details for this biographical sketch derive mainly from Furlong (1985), *Merton: A Biography*; Jim Forest (1991), *Living with Wisdom: A Life of Thomas Merton*; and Thomas Merton (1948), *The Seven Storey Mountain*.
3 A transcript of his notes for the lecture is found in Merton 2005. I have also used here my own transcriptions of the lecture tapes available from the Merton Foundation under the title 'Credence Cassettes'. Where I have drawn on his lecture notes I state this.
4 '*Quidquid enim anima nostra ante orationis horam conceperit, necesse est nobis per recordationem occurrere in ipsa oratione. Quamobrem quales volumes inveniri orantes, tales debemus nos praeparare ante tempus orationis.*'
5 See also Merton 1985, p. 568: 'Cassian is clearly not deep enough in his idea of "purity of heart"', letter to D. T. Suzuki, 30.11.59.

6

Living a Mindful Life: the Indian Tradition

Night Visit

Lord Yama visited me last night
And laid out the robes of death.
Invited to dance,
I hesitated –
Was it my time so soon?
Yet the moment I began the measure
Unworldly peace descended.[1]

The young poet steps out

In late 1882 a young 21-year-old Bengali man was trying to find his way in the world and his own voice. Born into a rich and impressive family there were high expectations of what he should achieve and, after several false starts, he really was not sure which path lay open to him in life. At this time, staying in a rented house in the European quarter of Calcutta at Sudder Street with his brother, a remarkable event overtook him one morning. He described it thus 30 years later:

> The end of Sudder St, and the trees on the Free School grounds opposite, were visible from our Sudder St house. One morning I happened to be standing on the verandah looking that way. The sun was just rising through the leafy tops of the trees. As I gazed, all of a sudden a lid seemed to fall from my eyes, and I found the world bathed in a wonderful radiance,

with waves of beauty and joy swelling on every side. The radiance pierced the folds of sadness and despondency which had accumulated over my heart, and flooded it with universal light. (Tagore 1917/1991, pp. 153–4)

This account, from Rabindranath Tagore's autobiographical collection *My Reminiscences* (*Jibansmriti*), was written by the 50-year-old poet in 1911. Almost 20 years later – in 1930 – as he approached 70, he reflected again on the experience for an audience at Oxford University. By now it was nearly 50 years after the event, but it had clearly lost none of its youthful vigour and power:

One day while I stood watching at early dawn the sun sending out its rays from behind the trees, I suddenly felt as if some ancient mist had in a moment lifted from my sight, and the morning light on the face of the world revealed an inner radiance of joy. The invisible screen of the commonplace was removed from all things and all men, and their ultimate significance was intensified in my mind; and this is the definition of beauty. (Tagore 1931/1988, p. 58)

The event, whatever it was, was clearly the point at which the young poet's life was consecrated to a higher ideal. The two accounts, separated by 20 years, still speak of the urgency and power of this encounter. As Tagore himself acknowledged, it was the beginning of his adult life as a poet and from it one of his early great poems emerged: *The Awakening of the Spring* (*Nirjharer Swapnabhanga*):

How have the sun's rays in my heart
Entered this morning! How have the songs
Of morning birds into the dark cave broken!
Who knows why, after long, my soul has woken!
The soul awakes, the waters stir:
I cannot stem my heart's passion, my heart's desire ...

> So much of words, so much of song, so much of life have I.
> So much delight, so much desire – a heart in ecstasy.
> What can it mean? My soul today has woken after long ...
> What song have the birds sung today, what sunshine do I see.
> (Tagore 2004, pp. 45–6)

The joy of the young poet on the threshold of adult life reflects the joy we can experience from our first encounter with the Divine or transcendent other. Yet, the consequences of such an encounter may not be so easy to integrate into our wider lives. Indeed, it may sometimes take an entire life to achieve that. Accordingly, in this our final chapter we shall explore this lifelong process of integration, drawing particularly upon Tagore's experiences and those of his fellow Indian spiritual seekers, Christian and non-Christian.

In the above description the poet seems as surprised as anyone by what is happening and this leads me to the first point I want to make here. My contention is that all of us, whether we admit it or not, in our late teens/early twenties, like Tagore, encounter the numinous for the first time. This can be a moment of beauty and ecstasy as it was for Tagore (as evidenced by the long and fruitful artistic life he subsequently had) or, as is normally the case today, certainly in the West, it can be a moment of terror and trauma, sometimes even leading to psychosis, breakdown, drug addiction, or worse.

We may choose to engage in mindful or prayerful practices in our lives or not, but, I am arguing here, whether we like it or not the aspect of Reality greater than our small egos will sooner or later crash into our lives regardless of our personal practices. The genius of the great religious traditions we have been exploring in this book is that they provide the means and circumstances to integrate these experiences into our broader lives. They do not tame them or think them away, but respect their power and the need for us to recognize the transcendental polarity innate in our human nature.

In the two previous books I have written in this sequence

– *The Pursuit of the Soul* (Tyler 2016) and *Confession: The Healing of the Soul* (Tyler 2017a) – I have emphasized how in order to talk of this dimension of our reality, what we can call 'the soul', we must often have recourse to alternative modes of discourse – the poetic, the paradoxical, the mythological and the embodied. Thus, when we essay how different cultures have interpreted this 'transcendental encounter', we often find them resorting to these means.

In India there are the *Vedas*, the *Upanishads*, and the great tradition of Eastern wisdom to which I will return shortly. Where I come from – the Celtic fringes of Europe – we have something similar; we call them the Celtic-Christian myths and they arise at that point in the twelfth and thirteenth centuries when Europe as we know it is first emerging from the period of collapse after the end of the Roman Empire, sometimes called the Dark Ages.[2] From this time we have the first written examples of old stories that have clearly existed in oral form long before they were written down. One such story is the legend of Perceval – the young lad who runs away from his mother into the dark woods and encounters the Grail Castle. I mention this story for it directly mirrors the encounter with the 'Awakening Spring' experienced by Tagore and bears upon the theme of this chapter – how do we integrate the insights of contemplation and mindfulness into our ordinary lives?

Rudolf Otto, writing in *The Idea of the Holy* (1917), described one of the key attributes of the Divine as the *fascinans*, that which draws us to it – the others being the *tremendum* and *numens* – the terrifying fear and the otherness of the Divine. The young Perceval wandering in the forest encounters five noble knights who appear to him like beings from another realm. Five, the Quintessence, was the medieval symbol for that which transcends our ordinary life and world, bound by the traditional four elements of earth, wind, fire and water. This correctly describes the young person's encounter with the transcendent. As in the case of Tagore, it can literally blow our minds. The tragedy of human life, however, is that only in a very few cases can the young person hold the experience and build on it. In this respect I think that the people of India today are at an advantage to those of us in Europe. In India, respect is still given to the transcendental realities of life in a way that is becoming increasingly rare in the West (although even in sacred India a new wave of materialism is emerging). In the West today the transcendental is too often masked or perverted by gross consumerism into strange twisted ends. Young people still receive the transcendental encounter in the West (as they always have and presumably always will), but they have no categories to process it. So many times, as a psychologist, I receive cases of young people with drug, relationship, and depressive problems which at heart are psycho-spiritual issues rather than psychological or somatic issues alone. Like the young Perceval, they stumble into the Grail Castle – usually by accident – but they don't know what to do once they are in there.

In the legend, we hear that the young lad is asked the 'Grail question' at the climax of the Ceremony of the Grail Castle: 'What is the meaning of the Grail? Whom does it serve?' Terrified out of his wits, the boy, as the Americans say, 'drops the ball'. He cannot answer the question and the castle immediately vanishes. As the American psychologist Robert Johnson writes:

> The most important event of one's inner life is portrayed in the story of the Grail Castle. Every youth blunders his or her way into the Grail Castle sometime around age 15 or 16 and has a vision that shapes much of the rest of their life. Like Parsifal, they are unprepared for this and do not have the possession to ask the question that would make the experience conscious and stable within them. (Johnson 1989, p. 47)

The majority of us are not Tagores. We receive the experience but we do not necessarily instantly begin writing Nobel award-winning poetry. Rather, we are left with a confused mess. These are really deep transcendental changes the young person is undergoing. They do not really know what is happening and, I'm afraid, neither often do those who are meant to guide them! To work with such people requires a bypassing of the ego – a real exercise in Christian humility as we allow the Holy Spirit to take root in the person's life.

If this encounter is botched or disrupted (as is sadly too often the case today), the seeker – like Perceval – can spend the next 20 years in the spiritual wilderness – and it will lead to a lifetime of bitterness and misery. If not handled correctly the wound can last for decades afterwards, curdling someone's appreciation of religion – and ultimately life itself. Perceval himself will spend 20 years after his botched encounter with the Grail, struggling and wandering – trying to find the Castle again but never able to do so.

We could say, then, that the spiritual search often begins with a call – what has traditionally been called by Christians 'a vocation'. How we respond to that is up to us. Likewise, when people today, especially young people, embark upon the path of mindfulness there is often a great deal of guidance at the beginning, but what if such a person, during their practice, breaks through into the transcendent realm – the Grail Castle? This is often where more guidance is needed and, fortunately, turning to the Indian tradition, this can be found.

The fourfold path

We began this chapter with the 70-year-old poet reflecting at Oxford University on his life in the 1930 Hibbert lectures subsequently published as *The Religion of Man*. As he looked back on his long and productive life in these lectures Tagore drew upon the ancient Indian classification of the fourfold stages of life, when he said: 'as the day is divided into morning, noon, afternoon and evening so India had divided man's life into four parts' (Tagore 1931/1988, p. 123).[3] For the remainder of this chapter we shall consider this fourfold classification, drawing out from it how we can mindfully engage with the stages of life.

In early Sanskrit texts such as the *Upanishads* and the *Laws of Manu* human life is traditionally understood as lasting 100 years and being divided into four stages, or *āśrama*, of some 25 years each: *brahmacarya* (the initial period of discipline and studentship), *gṛhasta* (the householder stage), *vānaprastha* (loosening of bonds from the householder stage and preparation for old age) and, finally, *sannyāsa* – the absolute renunciation. As understood in the *Laws of Manu* and most early texts, these phases were usually limited to certain castes and often only men.[4] With this in mind let us look at the four stages in turn and see how they relate to the mindful approach to life as advocated throughout this book.

Brahmacarya (the initial period of discipline in education)

The first phase of life, what Tagore terms the *brahmacarya*, is what will hopefully prepare us for, and enable us to deal with, the consequences of that first early transcendental Grail encounter. We need, as I have said, this educational and noetic structure to make sense of the transcendent categories when they break into our lives at the end of adolescence and early adulthood. The university and the school give us very few answers, but hopefully they will prepare us sufficiently to recognize the right questions when they arise. As Tagore puts it: 'Our teachers, therefore, keeping in mind the goal of this progress, did not, in life's first stage of education, prescribe merely the learning of books or things, but *brahmacarya*, the living in discipline, whereby both enjoyment and renunciation would come with equal ease to the strengthened character'. (Tagore 1931/1988, p. 124).

In my experience, teaching spirituality and religion to young people in their late teens and early twenties is a strange business. On the one hand, they are preparing to go out into the burgeoning green sap of life, but on the other I am telling them that the truth lies elsewhere, not in iPhones, Xboxes, football and hot dates. How, then, can this ideal of renunciation be inculcated among young people? Tagore talks of the 'habituation of the mind' for the 'readiness of renunciation'. As we saw earlier, St Thomas Aquinas, 800 years ago, used much the same language when he spoke of the need to develop the *habitus* of virtue within the spiritual seeker. We must become accustomed, so wrote the Angelic Doctor, to the transcendent vision beyond the simple material perspective and, in one of the few occasions where St Thomas allows himself the liberty of a little joke, he puns that we attain this 'habit' of habitual action by putting on the 'habit' or cloak of the man-God Christ – even if the old Adam resists it.[5] In Tagore's words, we 'habituate the mind, from the very beginning, to be conscious of, and desirous of, keeping within the natural limits; to cultivate the spirit of enjoyment that is allied with the spirit of freedom, the readiness for renunciation' (Tagore 1931/1988, p. 124). In the context of this book, we could say that we consecrate our desires, positive and negative, to accustom them to seeking the transcendent. Today there is a great deal of effort put into introducing mindfulness into schools and there is no doubt that inculcating the habits of mindfulness, prayer and contemplation among young people will certainly bear great fruit later on. Cassian's 'purity of heart' and Merton's *'point vierge'* are second nature to young people. And indeed we could say that the susceptibility of young people to entering the 'Grail Castle' stems from the fact that in our early years we are closer to the original nature of the mind (and soul). These early encounters will remain so vivid and numinous for us for the rest of our lives because, essentially, at this point in our lives we encounter ourselves as we truly are. This is the mindful moment, so difficult to put into words and 'caught' rather than 'taught' through the poetic and mythological languages we have explored here.

Gṛhasta (a householder in the world)

Before we embark upon the second part of the journey – that of mid-life – it is worth highlighting one interesting aspect of Tagore's adolescent awakening with which we began the chapter. After he had experienced 'the awakening of the Spring' in a rather dull suburban street in Calcutta, his brother suggested that they might journey to the majestic Himalaya at Darjeeling for a holiday. 'So much the better', thought the poet, 'on the vast Himalayan tops I shall be able to look more deeply into what has been revealed to me in Sudder Street' (Tagore 1991, p. 154). Yet, as he rather nicely put it, 'victory lay in that little house in Sudder St ... I gazed at Kanchenjunga's grandeur against a cloudless sky, but there in what seemed to me the likeliest of places I found it not.' Tagore concludes, 'He who is the Giver can vouchsafe a vision of the eternal in the dingiest of lanes, and in an instant of time' (Tagore 1991, p. 156). Strangely enough, the same incident occurs to our young knight Perceval. Having encountered the Grail Castle as a young man he wanders aimlessly around seeking the Divine in the likeliest of places – rather like Tagore in his Himalayan settings. Yet, for 20 years, nothing is revealed to him. This, then, is the second point I want to make here concerning the stages of a mindful life: our life of mindfulness may be conceived in the ecstasy of the transcendental encounter of the young person, but it is in the boredom of the routine and the everyday that it will have to be worked out. The Grail Castle may take 20 years before it emerges again, often as spontaneous and as unexpected as its first appearance. Robert Johnson calls these years the 'dry years of a person's middle age. He knows less and less why he is functioning and is apt to give an evasive answer when asked about the meaning of his life' (Johnson 1989, p. 73).

This second phase in the traditional Indian schema is called that of the *gṛhasta*, the householder, which would correspond to these years – the 'dry years of the Western midlife'. As the

American Buddhist John Kornfield puts it, 'after the Ecstasy comes the laundry!' (Kornfield 2000). When discussing this phase Tagore quotes Manu with approval: 'It is not possible to discipline ourselves so effectively if we are out of touch with the world, as whilst pursuing the world-life with wisdom' (Tagore 1931/1988, p. 124). As with Perceval in his Grail search, the awakened spirit can only come to fruition, to reality, through the living out of 'work, especially good work', says Tagore, for it 'becomes easy only when desire has learnt to discipline itself. Then alone does the householder's state become a centre of welfare for all the world, and instead of being an obstacle, helps on the final liberation' (Tagore 1931/1988, p. 125). This is the self-same movement we have encountered in both Teresa of Avila and Thomas Merton when they urge the one engaged in contemplation to come into deeper engagement with the world around them.

If we engage in the mid-life Grail quest actively and mindfully, then rather than being a chore or a drudge the work will become the place of encounter with the Divine. These are Teresa's 'good works' and Merton's engaged social encounters for justice. We shall find the Grail 'just down the road at the second drawbridge on the left'. Indeed, in Vedic tradition, as Thottakara points out, the phase of the householder is one of the most revered as they are the ones who protect and nourish people at all the other three phases, providing a safe and stable environment within which the other spiritual work can take place (Thottakara 2009, p. 566). As it is stated in the *Laws of Manu*: 'Of all these four the householder, who performs Vedic and *Smṛti* rituals, is the noblest. He indeed protects all the other three. As the rivers find their rest in the ocean, so all the states of life find their support in the householder' (Thottakara 2009, p. 567). Thus, contemporary mindfulness practices, with their emphasis on pursuing the ordinary through our everyday encounters, would seem ideally suited to this second householder phase.

Yet, towards the end of this period old mortality will

begin to make its presence felt, ushering in the third and final periods, *vānaprastha*, or the loosening of bonds, and *sannyāsa*, the expectant awaiting of freedom at death. For these two final stages to happen, however, we need to learn the art of surrender and, for those of us who are engaged in active busy lives or surrounded by families, this is not so easy. This is the point that is often called the 'mid-life crisis' and it is worth pausing for a moment to reflect on the relationship between mindful contemplation and the mid-life crisis.

Interlude: the mid-life crisis

The first thing to note about this stage is that not everyone reaches it. According to the American psychologist James Fowler, the early phases of faith development have to establish prior boundaries and solidities before the phase of mid-life can be entered into. At this point the person becomes his or her own judge rather than relying on the thoughts and opinions of others. Previous symbols, rituals and myths are now questioned and 'demythologized'. There is a great deal of emphasis on the literal and cognitive and less emphasis on the intuitive, emotional and unconscious. Therefore, the end of this phase (the so-called 'mid-life crisis') is marked by emotional burnout due to the inability of the person to sustain the energy to maintain the boundaries of the self on this level: 'the wear and tear of maintaining personal boundaries,' writes Fowler, 'without access to the "heart" they suppressed in adopting the parental or cultural programme, becomes a serious drain' (Fowler 2000, p. 63).

The American Carmelite Jack Welch OCD makes a comparison here with the movement from the third to the fourth 'mansions' of Teresa of Avila's *Interior Castle* (Welch 1982; see also Tyler 2013). As Teresa herself says, the Third Mansion is characterized by the limits of what we can do by our own actions to render God's presence in our lives, but from the

Fourth Mansion onwards it is a matter of *surrender, letting go*, and 'letting God be God'. Although we may have had the transcendental encounter as young people, we may have not really assimilated its message. We entered the Grail Castle but we didn't ask the right question or receive the right answer. So, as we progress through early adult life, the wound that beset us early on begins to fester and poison. Therefore, the onset of the transition from early adulthood to middle adulthood is often marked by emotional burnout, neurosis, exhaustion, and collapse of values – this is the 'mid-life desert'. It is the time for the contra-psychological to emerge: the executive ego must begin to surrender control to the unconscious and suppressed. In Jungian terms, it is the time of integration of the shadow, the contra-sexual, and the archetype of the self. Fowler is not alone in stressing that this phase of our life calls for the 'nurturing methods of meditation, contemplation and therapy that nurture a safe permeability of the defensive membrane that separates conscious from unconscious' (Fowler 2000, p. 72). In other words, we need to be given a safe space where we can explore what has been suppressed during our earlier developmental phases. Interestingly enough, Jung sees the churches as the ideal container for this transition and, in his essay *The Stages of Life*, suggests that the churches have held the wisdom of containing this transition for centuries:

> Wholly unprepared, we embark upon the second half of life. Or are there perhaps colleges for forty-year-olds which prepare them for their coming life and its demands as ordinary colleges introduce our young people to a knowledge of the world? ... Our religions were always such schools in the past, but how many people regard them like that today? How many of us older ones have been brought up in such a school and really prepared for the second half of life, for old age, death and eternity? (Jung 1971, p. 398)

A key dimension of this phase, which holds for people of faith as well as those engaged in secular therapies, is the acknowledgement of the spiritual dimension of the person. The therapies of middle age, for Fowler, 'cannot do their work without acknowledging the spiritual nature of the task, and without reliance upon a spirit of love and acceptance, of healing and forgiveness beyond the power of humans alone' (Fowler 2000, p. 74).

In contrast to the certainties of early adulthood, the onset of middle adulthood is a time when we are required to develop what Fowler calls 'epistemological humility' (Fowler 2000, p. 72). In Jung's words, 'what was great in the morning will be little in the evening, and what in the morning was true will at evening have become a lie' (Jung 1971, p. 399). This is a period in a person's life that calls for the appreciation of paradox, mystery, and what de Cusa calls the 'coincidence of opposites' – the *coincidentia oppositorium* (see Fowler 2000, p. 71).

Fortunately, from the point of view of psychological health, as we have seen throughout this book, Christian tradition has well-established resources for navigating this particularly tricky stage of life, which is why Jung acknowledged the importance of such religious traditions. The present book is intended as the third and final part of a trilogy that began in 2016 with *The Pursuit of the Soul*. I ended that first book by suggesting five aspects of 'soul-making' as we encounter the realm I am describing here: the need for a new perspective; the move into cognitive uncertainty; the importance of ambiguity and paradox; the return of the artistic and creative potential; and reconnection with the relational and libidinal (see Tyler 2016, pp. 177–9). I am suggesting now, as I conclude this trilogy, that for all who embark on the mindful life of contemplation – whether that is through traditional religious paths such as Christianity or Buddhism, or through contemporary means such as mindfulness – there will come a point when the small everyday ego must step aside to make way for a larger sense of self. In the Christian tradition (the perspective I am writing from here) this will by necessity include an encounter with the transcendent realm. However, even in the Buddhist and mindfulness traditions too, I would argue, there will come a point when the small everyday ego will be challenged to contemplate its place in the cosmos. As the mindfulness movement is still relatively young it may take a few years more for this to become apparent, but if the lessons of the older world religions are taken seriously then an entrance into the Grail Castle will at some point be inevitable and, as always when one stumbles into an unexpected social situation, it is often a good idea to be prepared in advance!

Thus, the mid-life phase is the moment of Cusa's *Coincidentia Oppositorium* – the holding together of the opposites in mystery and paradox. But, as I have argued here, not necessarily on the mystical plains of the Himalayan heights, but rather the 'balancing of heaven and earth' as we find the extraordinary in the everyday – a balance I have emphasized throughout this book.

In the legend of Perceval, having fluffed his early encounter and having wandered aimlessly for 20 years, he suddenly finds the Grail Castle again. But this latter, as it were 'mid-life' encounter happens not in some grand and reverent setting but in the most ordinary and everyday fashion. As Johnson puts it, it happens 'just down the road, turn left, and over the drawbridge' (Johnson 1989, p. 43). The Divine is now to be found in the ordinary and the everyday or, as Teresa of Avila says, 'amongst the pots and pans' (*The Book of Foundations* 5.8).

The old fool Perceval can witness the Grail Ceremony again. However, this time he is ready for the questions. Having gone through the gruelling 20 years in the wilderness of mid-life tribulations, doing his mindfulness meditation in the world and living out his desert spirituality, he is ready now for the second great encounter in his life with the transcendental. This time he can answer the question, 'What is the meaning of the Grail? Whom does it serve?' As Johnson paraphrases it, 'Where is the center of gravity of a human personality; or where is the center of meaning in a human life?' (Johnson 1989, p. 77). For this is the great question of mid-life that is posed to us all – 'What is the meaning of our life? Whom does it serve?'

Those who have not engaged in mindfulness or contemplation might say that the meaning lies in *me, the ego, the self* – *I* am searching for *my* happiness. Yet the answer Perceval now gives, after his life of tribulation, is 'The Grail serves the Grail King' – the centre of human existence lies in the transcendent. Through our life of ordinary acts of loving-kindness we have shifted the centre of the personality away from our own small and limited perspective to the wider perspective of the Divine. As Johnson puts it: 'the object of life is not happiness, but to serve God' – the Grail King – 'all of the Grail quests are to serve God' (Johnson 1989, p. 79).

Mid-life, then, far from being a dead-end or desert, ends up as being a privileged locus of encounter with the Divine – as it was for our desert elders all those years ago. If we have followed faithfully and mindfully the complicated psycho-spiritual changes of these years, and if we have maintained the correct awareness of the transcendent in balance with the demands of our place in our community, family and society, then this period can be uniquely enriching and rewarding. Either way, the foundations are laid for the third and final stage of life: late adulthood and old age.

Vānaprastha (the loosening of bonds)

In his earlier essay of 1924, 'The Fourfold Way of India', written when he was in his early sixties, Tagore makes a strong contrast between the Western and Eastern approaches to life. 'In Europe,' he writes, 'we see only two divisions of man's worldly life – the period of training and that of work. It is like prolonging a straight line till, wearied, you drop off your brush' (Tagore 1996, p. 498). For, as he points out, 'work is a process and cannot really be the end of anything' and yet 'Europe has omitted to put before man any definite goal in which its work may find its natural termination and gain its rest'. India, on the other hand, 'has not advised us to come to a sudden stop while work is in full swing' (Tagore 1996, p. 499). This is where the account of the third and fourth stages of life differs so markedly from the dominant narrative currently apparent in the West – that we prepare ourselves for work (schools and universities being the places to acquire the necessary skills for a life of work), we work (the most important part of our life), and then (if we are lucky) we 'retire' or, as Tagore puts it, 'drop off our brush' to fill the final years watching daytime TV or visiting the grandchildren. By contrast, what Tagore presents us with in the third and fourth stages of life is the deliberate and calculated move to renunciation that is enshrined in the Indian tradition. 'After the infant leaves the womb,' writes Tagore, 'it still has to remain close to its mother for a time, remaining attached in spite of its detachment' (Tagore 1931/1988, p. 125), until, that is, it can accustom itself to its new phase.

In his spiritual autobiography, Rabindranath Tagore's father, Debendranath Tagore, describes a strange incident. As a young man (as many young men tend to), he had led a somewhat dissolute life. At a bleak period of his young life, having lost his beloved grandmother, he had turned away from his former pleasures but found no satisfaction either in the practices or scriptures of the great religions. One day 'all of a sudden', as he wrote, 'I saw a page from some Sanskrit book flutter past me. Out of curiosity I picked it up but found I could understand nothing of what was written on it' (Kripalani 1997, p. 7). Finally, a well-known Sanskrit scholar was sent for and he interpreted it as the opening verse of the *Isa Upanishad*: 'All this, whatever moves in this moving world, is enveloped by God. Therefore renounce and enjoy; do not covet what belongs to others' (*Isa Upanishad* 1). The power of this verse was so strong that he began the process of renouncing his wealth and former sensual life to engage in the practices of prayer and almsgiving while remaining a householder with many responsibilities to his family and estates. In a similar spirit, his son, after his experience at Sudder Street, realized a similar 'habituation of mind' to 'renounce and enjoy'. In Tagore's schema, as we embark on the third stage of life, we begin to allow this loosening and renunciation to become the norm in our lives.[6]

At this stage, Tagore writes, the seeker 'still gives to the world from his store of wisdom and accepts its support' but there is a lack of intimacy, vigour and concern – as was the case in the householder phase 'there being a new sense of distance' (Tagore 1931/1988, p. 125). We are quite literally loosening our bonds to the world around us as we prepare for the final great journey upon which we can take nothing with us. What is noticeable in this third phase, in contrast to what we have heard before, is that this third and the subsequent final phase, *sannyāsa*, expectant awaiting of freedom across death, are clearly phases of withdrawal from life and its engagements. Re-entering the Grail Castle and re-situating the ego, we are enjoined, following Christian gurus such as Teresa of Avila and Thomas Merton, to engage in union with action in the world. Tagore's final schema, on the other hand, is one of withdrawal and solitude.

Can the two, then, be reconciled: the Indian withdrawal from the world and the Christian life of active holiness? At first sight this seems a most problematic juxtaposition. Yet, I think the two can be reconciled, as I shall try to show.

As we have seen, even in Tagore's own writing on the fourfold stages of life there exists a tension and contradiction often reflecting his own mood and attitude to his own life at the time of writing. When he got around to writing about the phases of life in his late publication *The Religion of Man*, being nearly 70 he felt able to give due weight to each of the phases and their importance in individual development. Yet, as a young man writing in 1892 in his early thirties and a decade after the Sudder Street revelation with which we began this chapter, he made an interesting remark referring to the final stage of renunciation – the *sannyāsa*: 'If by nature I were a *sanyasi*, then I would have spent my life pondering life's transcience, and no day would have gone by without a solemn rite to the glory of God. But I am not, and my mind is preoccupied instead by the beauty that disappears from my life each day; I feel I do not appreciate it properly.'[7] And, a year later he added: 'There are two aspects to India: the householder and the *sanyasi*. The first refuses to leave his home hearth, the second is utterly homeless. Inside me both aspects are to be found.'[8] I think that it is in this 'creative unity' with which Tagore expressed his life that we find the 'coincidence of opposites' that could best characterize the 'Christian *sannyāsi/ini*'.

The latter phase of life has increasingly become in the West a conflict and struggle with death as we slump on the sofa after a life of hard work. Hermann Hesse, the Swiss poet, saw the art of life as the art of befriending death and, as Tagore famously put it, death is simply the lowering of the lamps as the dawn approaches. In the Oxford Lectures, he described death as 'the truth that comes as conqueror only because we have lost the art of receiving it as guest' – this is St Francis of Assisi's 'sister death' so beautifully described in *Laudato si'*.[9] Levinson talks of a 'Late Adult Transition' in the early sixties that prepares the way for this phase (Levinson 1986, p. 120). As we have seen, the preceding mid-life phase had prioritized the need to embrace paradox and embrace the opposite. At this later point, however, the de-centring of the early adult ego that has been occurring for the past 20 to 30 years now reaches its culmination and, consequently, a certain peace returns.

Sannyāsa (the final renunciation)

This final phase, what Fowler terms 'Universalizing Faith', is marked with an increasing need to place the hard-won revelations of middle age at the service of the world (Fowler 2000, p. 75). Perceval's displaced ego is now put at the service of the Grail. After the mystical ecstasies of the *Interior Castle*, St Teresa of Avila, as we have seen, exhorts her nuns to return to 'Good works! Good works!' Clearly, in the Christian tradition, following the practice of Christ, the ageing Christian soul must now remain in service in the world. Yet, where I think writers like Tagore and John of the Cross are valuable is that they remind us that this final stage moves beyond the purely psychological. For, as the outer forms die, we move into a new place – a poetic place beyond the psychological and even the theological. As Pope Francis says, a new child is born as we are called out of the caves of our comfort zones (Pope Francis 2014, p. 45). The Indian Carmelite priest Kurian Perumpallikunnel CMI suggests that Indian *sannyāsa* is one of renunciation without restriction (Perumpallikunnel 2009, p. 680); the emphasis is on the individual relationship with God mediated by the guru and what we find there is little emphasis on communitarian prayer such as the Eucharist as found in the Christian tradition. Yet, in spite of the differences, it is possible to see both Indian *sannyāsa* and Christian contemplative life as two aspects of the final encounter and relationship with the ultimate goal of human life – our encounter with the limit of human mortality and the embrace of Sister Death.

Over the years, during my many visits to India, I have had the great privilege of encountering just such Indian Christian *sannyāsis/inis*. Such Christian renouncers may adopt the life of wandering ascetics, such as the late Swami Sadanand, or settle in an ashram as did Fr Thomas Kochumuttom CMI, the guru of the Jeevan Dhara ashram in the Himalayas, or Fr Francis Vineeth CMI, the founder of the Vidyavanam ashram in Karnataka. Among women *sannyāsinis* the same variation is seen between those who start ashrams such as Vandana Mataji (founder of Jeevan Dhara where Fr Thomas is now the guru), forest dwellers such as Prasanna Devi of Rajkot, Gujarat and Paulina, a wandering *sannyāsini* of Rishikesh. For Fr Perumpallikunnel, *sannyāsa* is a matter of right relationship with God and the world – he compares it to Ignatian 'indifference' where a compassionate attitude is adopted towards all people and all things. In this respect, for him right disposition is the most important thing rather than the actual circumstances of one's existence.[10] For Fr Kochumuttom, all Christians consecrated to the religious life are, by definition, *sannyāsis/sannyāsinis*, yet he distinguishes the Christian path from that of, say, Hindu or Buddhist asceticism, as a work of collaboration between the seeker and God. The seeker must undergo the necessary ascetic training or *tapas*, but they must also be cognisant, as Christians, that such spiritual attainment is dependent upon the action and collaboration with God. What is good in the non-Christian traditions should be adopted, he advises, but always with right discernment to the wider Christian perspective.[11]

Writers such as Paul Pattathu have stressed the need for Christian *sannyāsa* to take place within the context of a Christian ashram (see Pattathu 1997). Again, influenced and developed by pioneers such as Henri le Saux (Abhishiktananda), Bede Griffiths, Jules Monchanin and Francis Acharya, the Christian ashram movement has grown considerably in India in recent years. The ashram itself, as practitioners such as Fr Thomas Kochumuttom describe it, is based on ancient Indian spiritual traditions but has at its heart two basic foundations. First, in keeping with the Indian tradition it is based on the spiritual example of individuals – the original guru or holy man/woman – rather than the rules and regulations of an institution. Second, it reflects in its everyday life the values and culture of 'village India' (Kochumuttom 2015, p. 46). Clearly influenced by the pioneering work of Abhishiktananda (not least in the ashram liturgy which incorporates texts and *bhajans* written by the Swami), Fr Kochumuttom adds an extra dimension to Abhishiktananda's three guiding values of silence, simplicity and solitude – namely, openness.[12] In contrast to the Benedictine tradition from which Abhishiktananda came, Fr Kochumutton sees in the ashram 'no place for enclosures'.[13] For him, 'there is nothing either in the persons or the house or the personal rooms that others should not come to know and understand' (Kochumuttom 2015, p. 46) so that 'one is ready to open one's heart or mind' (as well as one's room) to anyone who asks, which requires 'utter honesty and transparency, sincerity and straightforwardness'. On a practical level the ashram should be furnished simply with cheap furniture and fittings – which would neither be attractive to potential thiefs nor require much money to replace if stolen! At Jeevan Dhara ashram Fr Kochumuttom puts this practice into action and, with the three other virtues of silence, solitude and simplicity, creates a stable and peaceful environment where the contemplation of the divine *sat-cit-ānanda* can proceed day and night.[14]

Religious or lay, the stable environment of the Christian ashram, centred on the liturgy and the teaching of the guru, seems to offer a secure place where the more wayward demands of *sannyāsa* can be practised. Christians practising *sannyāsa* in India today have learnt that the 'further shore' of *sannyāsa*, when it is practised in a Christian context, needs to be held by the context and support of the ashram or wider religious community. In the Indian tradition, the *sannyāsi* 'owns no place and no person and has to be by definition a solitary wanderer' (Thottakara 2009, p. 561). The Christian, in contrast, by virtue of their consecration to Christ, remains in service to the world even though they do not identify with the world's goals and aims.[15] Thottakara calls it 'the Yoga mind' that integrates apparently bi-polar realities, and he mentions Fr Francis Vineeth as an example of a modern *sannyāsi* 'who tries to awaken the religious-spiritual consciousness of the *sadhakas* and develop in them a soul culture that is deeply rooted in the age-old principles of Indian spirituality and in the immensely rich Christian spiritual traditions without at the same time negating the positive values of matter, body and this world' (Thottakara 2009, p. 558). Which is not to say that there is no longer any room for the wandering Christian ascetic in today's modern India.

Nowhere is this better illustrated than in the rich life of Swami Sadanand, a Christian *sannyāsi*, who died in 2016. This remarkable Christian ascetic had spent his whole life, since taking the robe of a *sannyāsi*, pursuing justice and truth for the poorest and most alienated in India while also practising the deep ascetic and meditational life of a *sadhu*. He famously befriended the murderer of a Catholic nun, Sr Rani Maria, while the murderer served his time in prison so that when he was released, and repented of his crimes, he was accepted into the late nun's family. Such was the fame of this reconciliation that Pope Francis invited Swami Sadanand, the nun's murderer, and family to Rome in 2014. I had the great good fortune to meet Swamiji shortly before his death and his presence and life were indeed a convincing testimony to the possibility of Christian *sannyāsa* in the twenty-first century. To experience his smile, won despite a lifetime of hardship and suffering, was to experience the loving blessing of the Saviour.

At heart, then, what Indian *sannyāsa* and Christian spiritual life have in common is that for both renunciation, whether of the world or the ego, must be connected with love and surrender to the Creator. In this way, both Indian and Christian traditions embrace.

A mindful end

I mentioned earlier that, in Hermann Hesse's words, we must master in the second half of our lives the 'art of dying'. During the writing of this book I had the great privilege of sitting mindfully with a dear friend as he passed away. Of course it is difficult to write about mindful dying from the perspective of one in his mid-fifties. Yet, as my dying friend moved from one stage to the next of the dying process I was reminded of the ancient arts of dying as described in Tibetan, Egyptian and ancient Christian texts. At this point all science, and even theology comes to an end. As we saw when we discussed John of the Cross earlier, conceptual discourse gives way to poetry and song. For him, it is the time of the 'guiding night', the 'night more lovely than the dawn'. As he writes in *The Dark Night of the Soul*:

O guiding night!
O night more lovely than the dawn!
O night that has united
the Lover with the beloved one,
transforming the one into the other.
(DN: 5)

This is a 'song of the soul's happiness' as the soul passes into 'union with the beloved'. This is no depression or suicidal imagery. This is the ecstatic voice of one who has reached the furthest limits of human existence. The entry of the 'Dark Night', John tells us, is not a time for going over past sins and mistakes; it is rather a time 'to give comfort and encouragement that they may desire to endure this suffering as long as God wills, for until then no remedy – whatever the soul does, or the confessor says – is adequate' (A: 1.5).

As reflected in the works of John of the Cross and Tagore, this final stage of a life lived mindfully can, thus, only really be understood poetically. Fowler, Freud and Jung must all fall silent at this point. The dark night of the final stage of life is for John of the Cross to be seen as a stage through which the soul journeys 'toward that divine light of perfect union with God which is achieved, insofar as it is possible in this life, through love' (A: Prologue 1).

The final act, then, if we have lived our life in fullest embrace and with full attentiveness, is not to become, as Shakespeare warned, some 'lean and slippered pantaloon' but rather to touch, as the artists depicted it and the poets whispered it, that ultimate horizon of the journey into the mystical embrace of death such that all the conceptual discourse of psychology, and even theology, must break apart so that we are left only with the words of the poets in our hearts and minds:

Child, don't you know who calls you lovingly?
Why this fear?
Death is just another name for what you call life,

Not an alien at all.
Why, come then and embrace her!
Come and Hold Her Hand![16]

Exercise Six: The Bliss of the Lord

> In order to begin to talk of these fourth mansions it is best that I do what I have done already – that is, to commend myself to the Holy Spirit and ask him to speak for me so that you may understand something of the matters that remain to be shown. For from hereon we encounter supernatural things which it is most difficult to explain unless His Majesty takes it in hand ...
>
> As these mansions are much closer to where the King lives, they have great beauty and there are things so delicate to see and understand there, which the understanding does not have the capacity to grasp. (St Teresa of Avila, *The Interior Castle*, 4.1.1–2)

We have spent much of this chapter discussing the limits of conceptual discourse about the soul and the point where words fail as we enter the 'Grail Castle'. With these words St Teresa commences the difficult task of completing the second half of her great work *The Interior Castle*. Using all her literary skills, Teresa has realized that the life of prayer has two halves – she compares it to the life of a silkworm which then becomes a butterfly. The first half of the prayer journey is one where our efforts are paramount; however, she also acknowledges that this too must come to an end.

As we have done so far in these exercises, we prepare the time and place, we choose our posture, we choose our prayer words, etc. However, as St Teresa recognizes, there comes a point where the rationally controlling ego must let go. As she says, the silkworm must die and the little white butterfly emerge. As usual with Teresa, her teaching has great psycho-spiritual verisimilitude for at some point in our prayer exercises we will need to encounter this other dimension. The following exercise is one I have done with groups over the years, and which may help to prepare us for the moment when the all-controlling ego lets go to enable the little butterfly to fly once again.

As before, we take the usual time and space to prepare ourselves. Once we are settled in our prayer position we take some time with the stillness exercises already used: breathing, body-awareness and the use of the prayer words. We are now going to pass through the seven energy centres of the body, known in India as the 'chakras' or 'wheels'. We begin with the root *chakra* located at the base of the spine where it joins the earth. Concentrate on this spot and note the texture, feel and energy of this point. Perhaps a colour comes to mind. This is our point of contact with the earth, so feel the support of the earth as she supports you and sustains you. As with all the energy centres, if you feel a block or feel uncomfortable, remember the heart exercise from the exercise in Chapter 5 and imagine the warm healing touch of Christ on that place. Allow Christ to place his hand gently on the area that needs healing.

Now move slowly to the next *chakra* – the spleen *chakra* located between the root *chakra* and the navel close to the genitals, kidneys and urinary area. Again take some time to feel the strength and energy of this area, and if a particular colour comes to mind note it. This is the place of procreation, sexuality and generation and, as before, if there are any wounds here invoke God's presence through either the breath of the Spirit or the gentle healing touch of Christ.

When you are ready, move to the navel *chakra* which is located two fingers below the navel. A source of great energy, this is the origin of anger and our 'gut feelings'. Strong emotions arise here, and notice the colour and texture of this area. As before, evoke the soothing healing power of Christ if there are wounds that need healing here, especially around anger or fear.

As we pass through the energy centres try and let the energy flow from one to another, so that the root energy coming from the earth passes through the spleen and navel to the next *chakra* we have already encountered – the heart *chakra*. As in the previous exercise in Chapter 5, note the warmth of God's presence here and love that is generated.

This in turn will lead to the throat *chakra* – here our private world meets the public one and the wordless is given voice. Feel the shape of your voice and your vocalization – if you want to make a sound here, please do so, perhaps one of the prayer words used in a previous exercise or a sacred hymn or mantra you know. Again imagine the touch of Christ if there are blocks here and allow the heart energy to flow through the throat to the sixth *chakra* – the third eye.

Positioned at the forehead this is the seat of our outer wisdom. Traditionally it is the place anointed by both Christians and Hindus alike after certain rituals. What can you see from it?

At this point imagine a bright star arising in consciousness: 'Christ is the morning star – behold he comes quickly'. As you enjoy the pale light of this star let it rise until it is hovering over the top of your head. This is the final *chakra*, the crown *chakra*, where the body meets the infinite source of love. Allow that intuitive love to flow down over your head – like oil running over you – refreshing and anointing.

Now slowly reverse the order; allow the light to move down through the third eye, from the head back into the body via the throat, then into the warmth of the heart, the seat of emotions in the navel, the source of generation in the spleen, and finally back to the earth and the mother who holds you.

Return to your breathing and slowly open your eyes, giving a short prayer of thanks as before.

o O o

Of all the exercises in this book, this is the most unpredictable. If the exercise produces unpleasant effects don't hesitate to terminate it – it is clearly not for you! Whole schools of *chakra* exercise have been developed and if you want to develop this further I suggest you find a serious instructor. I have practised a form of this for many years, both on my own and with groups, and have always found it cleansing and healing. If we have blocks in our psycho-spiritual make-up they will quickly become apparent in this exercise, helping us to identify the areas in our soul-body that need healing. Needless to say, this may sometimes take many years of patient practice and exercise.

Variations on the Exercise

As well as specific colours, each *chakra* is often associated with a particular sound. I have sometimes invited groups to vocalize these sounds as we move through the *chakras* together. It can be a moving and healing experience, enabling the healing energy of the spirit to flow through the body.

Similarly, you may want to paint or draw your prayer-*chakra* experiences after you have finished one exercise. Sometimes a whole prayer session can be spent on one *chakra* alone – especially if blocks arise there. Here it would be good practice to use the Ignatian imaginative exercise mentioned in the exercise in Chapter 5 and to feel the touch of Christ on the blocked area. Afterwards I would encourage you to chat with Christ about the blocks and see if he has any suggestions.

With all these *chakra* exercises keep yourself well grounded – feet on the floor, bottom on the chair at all times!

Notes

1 London, January 2017. 'As a Buddha, Manjushri draws on the boundless life of ultimate voidness or freedom. To confront Death, the archetype of boundedness, limitation, terminality, he manifested the form of Death magnified to infinity. Death (Lord Yama), a single egocentric God, was overwhelmed by the god of selflessness. Death saw himself endlessly mirrored back to himself, infinitely outnumbered by himself' (Rhie and Thurman 1991, p. 36).

2 For more on this, see Tyler 2016.

3 I shall draw mainly on chapter 14 of *The Religion of Man* here, entitled 'The Four Stages of Life'. However, much of the lecture as delivered at Oxford in 1930 had already been published in 1924, six years earlier, in *The Modern Review* under the title 'The Fourfold Way of India' (reprinted in *The English Writings of Rabindranath Tagore*, vol. 3, ed. S. Kumar Das, New Delhi: Sahitya Akademi, 1996). I shall refer to this essay where the two variants differ significantly.

4 See A. Thottakara, '*Sannyāsa*: Dynamics of a Life of Renunciation', in S. Chackalackal (ed.), *New Horizons of Indian Christian Living*, Bengaluru: Vidyavanam, 2009, p. 560.

5 St Thomas Aquinas, *Summa Theologicae*, 1a 2ae, pp. 49–54.

6 The renouncer typically makes five vows: *Ahimsa* – abstention from violence; *Satya* – abstention from falsehood; *Asteya* – abstention from theft; *Brahmacarya* – abstention from sexual pleasure; and *Aparigraha* – abstention from possession (Thottakara 2009, p. 573).

7 Letter to his nephew, 15 June 1892, from Shelidah, reprinted in Tagore 1991b, p. 68.

8 Letter to his nephew, 7 February 1893, in Tagore 1991b, p. 78.

9 *Laudato si'*: 'Be praised, my Lord, through our sister Bodily Death, from whose embrace no living person can escape.'

10 Personal communication with the author; see also Perumpallikunnel 2009, pp. 663–84.

11 Personal communication with the author; see also Kochumuttom 2015.

12 For more on the life and teachings of Swami Abhishiktananda, see Tyler 2017a.

13 For more on the life and journey of Henri le Saux/Swami Abhishiktananda, see Tyler 2017a.

14 'Being-Consciousness-Bliss', the traditional three aspects of the Divine in the Indian contemplative tradition; see Tyler 2017a.

15 Although, as Thottakara notes, in recent years Buddhists, Hindus and Jains have all taken to more communitarian models of *sannyāsa*, imitating in many ways Christian monastic models of service to the world, the poor and downtrodden (Thottakara 2009, p. 562).

16 R. Tagore, 'Endless Death', trans. K. Dyson, in *I Won't Let You Go: Selected Poems*. 'When a *sannyāsin* dies, no funeral rites are performed; there is no mourning' (Thottakara 2009, p. 572).

Epilogue

On seeing a bronze statue of the Buddha with a hand raised in blessing

Your hand of blessing gives peace to all dimensions, all dominions. You calm the fears of all beings – frightened animals, humans, devas and devils alike.

Wrapped around you, your garment, like a death shroud or a placenta, brings you to birth in this realm, while your existence ceases into eddies and ripples of photons and electrons. Dispersing again, leaving only the serene smile, hanging blessing in the air. Today the shroud wraps a human form.

All fragility and beauty of human life is held here – watched over by the serene smile of the infinite.

Above the smile the sparkling, glittering hair that catches the light in a thousand refracted images while the reassuring gesture faces us with the solemnity of death – a deep bell tolling a summons to repentance.

Founded and conceived in sixth-century Bihar, you have travelled the centuries to rest in New York – the guest of wealthy benefactors. Now you delight the crowds in London on this cold November afternoon. Calming their fears and ushering them into enlightenment with a gentle touch – your special gift.

For there is not love here – that would be too trivial a word – but rather Compassion. Compassion of the finite in embrace with the infinite. This all-seeing Bodhisattva watches all beings as they are created, flourish and pass away. As they cry out in terror the gentle hand is raised again and the smile gifts its benediction.

All beings become enlightened by a smile.[1]

Conclusions

It is time to draw a few of the threads of our discussion together. I began with the mindfulness revolution and suggested that rather than be afraid of it Christians should understand that mindfulness is, too, part of their tradition. Although it has not developed as in the Buddhist schools, and certainly would not have the same teleological aims of the Buddha's prescriptions on *sati*, it is none the less an essential part of what constitutes Christian prayer. On one hand, this should not be surprising. I have been engaged with Buddhist thought and thinking now for over 30 years and some years ago, having met a Catholic priest with similar interests, I asked him if it was possible to reconcile the two. 'Of course!' he replied without hesitation, 'to be a good human being is to be a good Buddhist!' It is in this spirit that I have since approached the teachings of the Buddha and indeed of contemporary psychology and mindfulness.

For me, true Christian prayer will always contain an element of mindfulness (Cassian's 'tranquillity of mind', Merton's 'clarity') but Christianity, being a religion based on devotion to the Divine as well as knowledge, must supplement 'bare awareness' with the devotional love of heartfulness. In fact, it could be argued that Christian prayer goes beyond mindfulness to the prayer of the heart which is why I, for one, will continue to use the term 'heartfulness' as central to the Christian notion of prayer. Christian mindfulness or, better, heartfulness is thus a form of prayer that is centred on the Trinitarian relationship between Christ, the Spirit and the Father which enables us to enact the Divine in our ordinary everyday lives. By entering into the Trinitarian conversation we experience the two axes of our existence at once: the transcendent-immanent relationship and the horizontal relationship with our fellow humanity and all creation around us. Christian mindfulness is no 'holy huddle' but a call to set out on the path of service that in some cases may demand the ultimate sacrifice. Prayer, mindfulness and contemplation are thus not 'add-ons' to the life of a Christian but are, in fact, what give those lives their very identity and meaning. Prayer ('Christian mindfulness') is often about doing the opposite of what we think. It is a contra-spiral, a sign of contradiction, a Sign of Jonah.

We can call Christianity a religion of 'mindful activity'. Christians may adopt the method of mindfulness, but always there must be a 'contemplation in action' centred on love for the Guru Jesus – crucified and resurrected. In the world we shall have, so we are told, much tribulation. Teresa compared life to a 'night in a bad inn' (CV: 40.9). Yet by practising the way of Christian mindfulness as I have outlined in this book, we can have a glimpse of the treasure hidden in the field, the pearl of great price.

Exercise Seven: Contemplation to Give Love

St Ignatius of Loyola ends his *Spiritual Exercises* with an ecstatic 'Contemplation to Attain Love'. Here is a part of it:

> I recall the gifts I have received, my creation, redemption and other gifts particular to myself, I will ponder with deep affection how much God our Lord has done for me, and how much he has given me ...
>
> I see how God dwells in all creatures, in the elements, giving them being, in the plants, in the animals – feeling in them, in humans giving them to understanding and so in me, giving me being, animating me, giving me feeling and understanding ...
>
> I will speak as one making an offering with deep affection: 'Take, Lord, and receive, all my liberty, my memory, my understanding and all my will – all that I have and possess ... Give me only your love and your grace that is sufficient for me.' (*Spiritual Exercises*, 1996, pp. 234–5)

In a similar spirit I usually end a retreat or set of exercises with a group with a 'Contemplation to Give Love'. Here it is:

Again, take the usual time to prepare yourself for the exercise. Make yourself comfortable – feet on the ground, bottom on the seat/floor, back straight. As before, spend some time with the breathing and body exercises we have already done. Now, as in previous exercises, move your awareness to the heart centre. As before, notice the feeling in that part of you and invite Jesus to bring his healing touch there. Feel the warm hand of Christ on your heart, giving you the love you need at this moment. When you are ready, I now want you to transfer that love to those around you. It may be people in your house or in the room, or it may be a close friend or family member. Picture that person in your mind's eye and give them the love and healing touch that you have received from Christ. Wish them all good things and that they will find the peace they are looking for.

Now I want you to extend that love and warm energy to all your family and friends. Bring each of them in turn into your mind's eye and transfer that love energy to them, wishing them all the best for their journey through life.

Now give that love energy to all your work colleagues, to those who live near you and those you may have met today. Again, picture them before you – whether you actually like them or not – and transfer this loving-kindness to them. Pray that they may prosper and have a good and fulfilling life. If at this point you recall someone to whom you have difficulty transferring this love, stay with them a while and – if necessary – ask Jesus to come and help you.

I want you now to transfer this love energy to all in your city, town or region. Again contemplate all these people – some being born today, some dying, some ill and sick, some just married or newly engaged. Those in happiness, those in despair – equally alike, transfer this loving-kindness to them, this heart-energy that they will find the peace they are looking for.

Now I want you to transfer this love across the world. In particular, bring before your mind all those trouble-spots in the world that you hear about on TV and on the radio. Bring those who are at war, who suffer in conflict, who have lost loved ones into your loving-kindness. Bring the leaders – religious and civic – into your concentration as you give your

EPILOGUE

loving heart-energy to them. Again, evoke the name of Jesus to be with them now in their hour of difficulty.

Now transfer the energy to all the animals and plants that surround you at this moment – the birds, insects, creatures and animals in your neighbourhood. Like St Ignatius, thank God for their being and transfer to them all loving-kindness for their peace and contentment.

Finally, like the saint, transfer this love to all the created elements around you. Thank God for the mystery of this fragile planet and pass the loving-kindness to the greater mysteries of God's love dwelling in all created elements.

Finish the exercise with a short prayer of thanksgiving before opening your eyes again.

o O o

The importance of this exercise is that it reminds us we are not alone. If spiritual exercises are leading to increased egoism, narcissism or self-absorption then, frankly, you have gone astray. It is worth recalling St Teresa of Avila's wise words on the subject once again:

> When I see people very diligently observing the sort of prayer that they have and being very wrapped up in it when they have it (for it seems that they will not let the thought move or stir in case they lose a small morsel of the *gusto* or devotion that they have had), I realize how little they understand of the road to the attainment of union. They think that the whole business lies in such things.
>
> No, sisters, no! The Lord desires works, and that if you see a sick woman to whom you can give some help, never be affected by the fear that your devotion will suffer, but take pity on her: if she is in pain you should feel pain too; if necessary, fast so that she may have your food, not so much for her sake as because you know that the Lord desires it. (*The Interior Castle*: 5.3.11)

All our prayer, mindfulness and contemplation must lead to action in the world. In fact, prayer has at its heart an essential ethical element. Prayer – or indeed mindfulness – on its own is useless, and in fact can lead to the opposite direction we are seeking. The best prayer or mindfulness is often attentive action in service of suffering humanity. But to discuss that would require another book ...

Happy Mindful Living!

Note

1 London, December 2012.

Acknowledgements

To write a book of this scope covering so many genres and styles always requires much work and help from a whole host of unsung heroes and heroines. My first gratitude is to my colleagues, friends and students of St Mary's University, Twickenham, who have engaged in many conversations concerning these issues and commented on sections of the book. I am indebted to Dr Maureen Glackin for study leave given for research that would end up in several parts of this book. I would also like to thank participants at numerous 'Christian mindfulness' workshops up and down the country whose responses have helped shape this text. I am also grateful to Canon Professor Christopher Cook, Professor Rupert Gethin, Abbot Christopher Jamison, Fr Thomas Kochumuttom, Archbishop Kevin McDonald, Dr Kurian Perumpallikunnel and Fr Ronald Rolheiser for reading and offering comments on the text. During the writing of the book I was grateful to be received at several ashrams in India. I thank in particular Fr Thomas and Fr Jim of Jeevan Dhara Ashram for allowing me to have an unforgettable stay there, as well as Fr Jojo at Rishikesh, which visit was enlightened by the wisdom and presence of Fr Yann Vangeux and Sr Paulina. Also many thanks to Fr Paulachan Kochappilly for his unending kindnesses. Fr Kurian was an uncomplaining guide during my visits to Kerala, and particular thanks to Fr George, Fr Ishanand, Br Augustine, Anandaji and Fr John of Kurisumala monastery, the Carmelites of Mary Immaculate, and Shanti Sadan Siddhashram for their warm hospitality. In Montserrat I thank Professor Elizabeth Harris and Professor Michiko Yusa for their kindnesses during my stay. I shared a working version of this book with the Carmelite sisters of Ireland during a formation week in Dublin, and I am grateful to them for their warm responses to the material and their help in formulating some of the ideas expressed here (and not least their prayers!) – especially Sr Monica, Sr Teresita, Sr Maire and Sr Thérèse-Marie.

I am immensely grateful to David Shervington and all at SCM Press for having the courage to propose this project and give unfailing support throughout.

The Tagore poem *Endless Death* is reproduced with the kind permission of Bloodaxe Books.

I would like to thank Fr Joy Elamkunnapuzha CMI for permission to use his painting of Christ Dedicating the Church to the Father for the cover of this book.

During the writing of this book two dear friends passed through the final mindful stages of dying as described in the book: Dharam Pal Deved and Fr James McCaffrey OCD. It is to these two wonderful human beings that I lovingly dedicate this book.

Bibliography

(Swami) Abhishiktananda/Henri le Saux (1974) *Guru and Disciple*, trans. H. Sandeman. New Delhi: ISPCK, 1974.
Ajahn Brahm (2016) *Kindfulness*. New York: Wisdom.
Allchin, A. M. (2006) 'Can We Do Wales Then?', *The Merton Journal* 13.2.
Allison Peers, E. – *see* St Teresa of Avila.
Alvarez, Tomás – *see* St Teresa of Avila.
Anālayo (2003) *Satipaṭṭhāna: The Direct Path to Realization*. Cambridge: Windhorse.
Andrés Martín, M. (1975), *Los Recogidos: Nueva Vision de la Mistica Española (1500–1700)*. Madrid: Fundación Universitaria Española, Seminario 'Suarez'.

Baker, R. and Henry, G., eds (1999) *Merton and Sufism: The Untold Story*. Louisville, KY: Fons Vitae.
Baraut, Dom Cipriano – *see* Cisneros.
Bhikku Bodhi (2011) 'What Does Mindfulness Really Mean? A Canonical Perspective', *Contemporary Buddhism*, vol. 12, no. 1, pp. 19–39.
Boyce, B., ed. (2011) *The Mindfulness Revolution: Leading Psychologists, Scientists, Artists, and Spiritual Teachers on the Power of Mindfulness in Daily Life*. Boston, MA: Shambala.
Bullivant, S. (2013) *Faith and Unbelief*. Norwich: Canterbury Press.

Cassian, John (1955–9) *Conférences*, ed. E. Pichery. SC: 42, 54, 64. Paris: Cerf.
—— (1997) *The Conferences*, ed. B. Ramsey. New York: Newman Press.
Chozen Bays, J. (2011) 'What is Mindfulness', in *The Mindfulness Revolution: Leading Psychologists, Scientists, Artists, and Spiritual Teachers on the Power of Mindfulness in Daily Life*, ed. B. Boyce. Boston, MA: Shambala.
Chryssavgis, J. (2003) *In the Heart of the Desert: The Spirituality of the Desert Fathers and Mothers*. Bloomington, IN: World Wisdom Press.

Cisneros, García de (1965) *Obras Completas*, ed. Dom Cipriano Baraut. Montserrat: Abbey Presses.

Clément, O. (2013) *The Roots of Christian Mysticism: Texts from the Patristic Era with Commentary*. New York: New City Press.

Cousins, L. (1989) 'The Stages of Christian Mysticism and Buddhist Purification: The Interior Castle of St. Teresa of Avila and the Path of Purification of Buddhaghosa', in *The Yogi and the Mystic – Studies in Indian and Comparative Mysticism*, ed. K. Werner. London: Curzon and Riverdale.

De Mello, A. (1984) *Sadhana: A Way to God, Christian Exercises in Eastern Form*. New York: Image.

—— (2010) *Seek God Everywhere: Reflections on the Spiritual Exercises of St Ignatius*, ed. G. O'Collins, D. Kendall and J. LaBelle. New York: Image.

Dunn, M. (2003) *The Emergence of Monasticism: From the Desert Fathers to the Early Middle Ages*. Oxford: Blackwell.

Efrén de la Madre de Dios and Otger Steggink – *see* St Teresa of Avila.

Evagrius of Pontus (1971) *Évagre le Pontique, Traité Pratique ou Le Moine*, ed. A. Guillaumont and C. Guillaumont. SC: 170, 171. Paris: Cerf.

—— (1981) *Evagrius Ponticus: Praktikos, The Chapters on Prayer*. Cistercian Studies no. 4, trans. J. Bamberger. Kalamazoo, MI: Cistercian.

Forest, J. (1991) *Living with Wisdom: A Life of Thomas Merton*. New York: Orbis.

Fowler, J. (2000) *Faithful Change: The Personal and Public Challenges of Postmodern Life*. Nashville, TN: Abingdon Press.

(Pope) Francis (2014) *Keep Watch: Year of Consecrated Life, A Letter to Consecrated Men and Women Journeying in the Footsteps of God*. London: Catholic Truth Society.

—— (2015) *Laudato si', On Care for Our Common Home*. London: Catholic Truth Society.

Furlong, M. (1985) *Merton: A Biography*. London: Darton, Longman and Todd.

Gethin, R. (2011) 'On Some Definitions of Mindfulness', *Contemporary Buddhism*, vol. 12, no. 1, pp. 263–79.

—— (forthcoming) 'Emptiness and Unknowing: An Essay in Comparative Mysticism', in *Studies in Early Buddhism in Memory of L. S. Cousins*, ed. P. Harvey and N. Appleton. London: Equinox.

Grayston, D. (1985) *Thomas Merton: The Development of a Spiritual Theologian*. New York: Edwin Mellen.

Heelas, P and L. Woodhead (2004) *The Spiritual Revolution: Why Religion is Giving Way to Spirituality*. London: Wiley-Blackwell.

Hopkins, G. M. (1953/1985) *Poems and Prose*, ed. W. Gardner. London: Penguin.

Hugh of Balma (1995) *Théologie Mystique*, trans. F. Ruello. Paris: Éditions du Cerf.

—— (1997) *The Roads to Zion Mourn*, trans. D. Martin, in *Carthusian Spirituality: The Writings of Hugh of Balma and Guigo de Ponte*. Mahwah, NY: Paulist.

(St) Ignatius of Loyola (1996) *Saint Ignatius of Loyola: Personal Writings* ed. J. Munitiz and P. Endean. London: Penguin.

—— (2014) *Obras: San Ignacio de Loyola*. Madrid: Biblioteca de Autores Cristianos.

Jamison, C. (2006) *Finding Sanctuary: Monastic Steps for Everyday Life*. London: Orion.

(St) John of the Cross (1979) *The Collected Works of St John of the Cross*, trans. K. Kavanaugh and O. Rodriguez. Washington: ICS.

—— (2002) *San Juan de La Cruz: Obras Completas*. Madrid: Biblioteca de Autores Cristianos.

Johnson, R. (1989) *He: Understanding Masculine Psychology*. New York: Harper.

Jung, Carl (1971/1999) *The Collected Works of C. G. Jung*, trans. R. Hull and H. Baynes. London: Routledge.

Kabat-Zinn, J. (1994/2013) *Full Catastrophe Living: Using the Wisdom of Your Body and Mind to Face Stress, Pain, and Illness*. New York: Random House.

Kavanaugh, K. and Rodriguez, O. – *see* Teresa of Avila and St John of the Cross.

Keating, T. (2017) *World Without End*. London: Bloomsbury.

Kochumuttom, T. (2015) *Christian Life Amidst Many Religions*. Bengaluru: Dharmaram.

Kornfield, J. (2000) *After the Ecstasy, the Laundry*. New York: Rider.

Kripalani, K. (1961/1997) *Tagore: A Life*. New Delhi: National Book Trust.

Levinson, D. (1986) *The Seasons of a Man's Life*. New York: Ballantine.

Mace, C. (2008) *Mindfulness and Mental Health: Therapy, Theory and Science*. London: Routledge.

Melloni, J. (2000) *The Exercises of St Ignatius Loyola in the Western Tradition*. Leominster: Gracewing.

Merton, T. (1948/1990) *The Seven Storey Mountain*. London: SPCK.
—— (1949) *Seeds of Contemplation*. London: Hollis and Carter.
—— (1953) *The Sign of Jonas*. London: Hollis and Carter.
—— (1961a) *Disputed Questions*. London: Hollis and Carter.
—— (1961/1999) *New Seeds of Contemplation*. London: Burns and Oates.
—— (1966) *Conjectures of a Guilty Bystander*. New York: Doubleday.
—— (1968a) *Faith and Violence*. Indiana: University of Notre Dame Press.
—— (1968b) *Zen and the Birds of Appetite*. Kentucky: Abbey of Gethsemani.
—— (1969) *The Climate of Monastic Prayer*. Shannon: Irish University Press.
—— (1973) *Contemplative Prayer*. London: Darton, Longman and Todd.
—— (1974) *The Asian Journal of Thomas Merton*, ed. N. Burton, P. Hart and J. Laughlin. London: Sheldon.
—— (1981) *Reflections on My Work*, ed. R. Daggy. London: Collins.
—— (1985) *The Hidden Ground of Love: The Letters of Thomas Merton on Religious Experience and Social Concerns*, ed. W. Shannon. New York: Farrar, Straus and Giroux.
—— (1994) *Witness to Freedom: Letters in Times of Crisis*, ed. W. Shannon. New York: Farrar, Straus and Giroux.
—— (1996) *The Journals of Thomas Merton 1960–1963: Turning Toward the World: The Pivotal Years*, ed. A. Kramer. London: Harper.
—— (1998) *The Journals of Thomas Merton 1963–65: Dancing in the Water of Life: Seeking Peace in the Hermitage*. San Francisco: HarperCollins.
—— (2003) *The Inner Experience: Notes on Contemplation*, ed. W. Shannon. London: SPCK.
—— (2004) *Peace in the Post-Christian Era*. New York: Orbis.
—— (2005) *Cassian and the Fathers: Initiation into the Monastic Tradition*, ed. P. O'Connell. Kalamazoo, MI: Cistercian Publications.
—— (2008) *Survival or Prophecy? The Correspondence of Jean Leclercq and Thomas Merton*, ed. P. Hart. Collegeville, MI: Liturgical Press.
Mitchell, D. and J. Wiseman (1999) *The Gethsemani Encounter: A Dialogue on the Spiritual Life by Buddhist and Christian Monastics*. New York: Continuum.

Nyanaponika Thera (1994) *The Power of Mindfulness: An Inquiry into the Scope of Bare Attention and the Principal Source of its Strength*. Kandy, Sri Lanka: The Buddhist Publication Society.

BIBLIOGRAPHY

O'Reilly, T. (1973) 'The Structural Unity of the *Exercitatorio de la Vida Spiritual*' in *Studia Monastica*, 15.
Osuna, Francisco de (1981) *Francisco de Osuna: The Third Spiritual Alphabet*, trans. M. Giles. New York: Paulist.
—— (1998) *Tercer Abecedario Espiritual de Francisco de Osuna*, ed. S. López Santidrián. Madrid: Biblioteca de Autores Cristianos.
Otto, R. (1917/1958) *The Idea of the Holy: An Inquiry into the Non-Rational Factor in the Idea of the Divine and its Relation to Rational*, trans. J. Harvey. Oxford: Oxford University Press.

Palma, Bernabé de (1998) *Via Spiritus*, ed. T. Martín. Madrid: Biblioteca de Autores Cristianos.
Pattathu, P. (1997) *Ashram Spirituality: A Search into the Christian Ashram Movement against its Hindu Background*. Indore: Satprakashan.
Perumpallikunnel, K. (2009) 'Mystical Experience: Fount and *raison d'être* of *sannyāsa*', in *New Horizons of Indian Christian Living*, ed. S. Chackalackal, pp. 663–84. Bengaluru: Vidyavanam.

Rhie, M. and R. Thurman (1991) *Wisdom and Compassion: The Sacred Art of Tibet*. New York: Harry Abrams.
Rhys Davids, T. W. (1881) *Buddhist Suttas*. Oxford: Clarendon.

Scharf, R. (2015) 'Is Mindfulness Buddhist? (and Why it Matters)', *Transcultural Psychiatry*, vol. 52, no. 4, pp. 470–84.
Shapiro, S. and R. Walsh (2006) 'The Meeting of Meditative Disciplines and Western Psychology: A Mutually Enriching Dialogue', *American Psychologist*, vol. 61 (3), April, pp. 227–39.
Sri Aurobindo (1971/1994) *The Upanishads*. Pondicherry: Sri Aurobindo Ashram.

Tagore, R. (1917/1991) *My Reminiscences*. London: Macmillan.
—— (1931/1988) *The Religion of Man*. London: Unwin.
—— (1991) *Glimpses of Bengal: Selected Letters by Rabindranath Tagore*, ed. K. Dutta and A. Robinson. London: Macmillan.
—— (1991a) 'Endless Death', trans. K. Dyson, in *I Won't Let You Go: Selected Poems*. Glasgow: Bloodaxe.
—— (1996) 'The Fourfold Way of India'. Reprinted in *The English Writings of Rabindranath Tagore*, vol. 3, ed. S. Kumar Das, New Delhi: Sahitya Akademi.
—— (2004) *Selected Poems of Rabindranath Tagore*, ed. S. Chaudhuri. Oxford: Oxford University Press.
(St) Teresa of Avila (1623) *The Flaming Hart, or, the life of the Gloriovs S. Teresa Foundresse of the Reformation of the Order of the All-*

immaculate Virgin-Mother, our B. Lady, of Mount Carmel, trans. Tobie Matthew. Antwerp: Joannes Meursius.

—— (1946) *The Complete Works of St Teresa of Jesus*, trans. E. Allison Peers, 3 vols. London: Sheed and Ward.

—— (1980–7) *The Collected Works of St Teresa of Avila*, trans. K. Kavanaugh and O. Rodriguez, 3 vols. Washington: ICS.

—— (1997) *Obras Completas de Santa Teresa de Jésus*, ed. Efrén de la Madre de Dios and Otger Steggink. Madrid: Biblioteca de Autores Cristianos.

—— (1998) *Santa Teresa Obras Completas*, trans. P. Silverio de Santa, ed. Tomás Alvarez. Burgos: Editorial Monte Carmelo.

Thanissaro, Bhikkhu (2010) 'Mindfulness Defined', in *Access to Insight*, http://www.accesstoinsight.org/lib/authors/thanissaro/mindfulnessdefined.html.

(St) Thomas Aquinas (1966) *Summa Theologiae*, ed. T. Gilbey. London: Eyre and Spottiswoode.

Thottakara, A. (2009) '*Sannyāsa*: Dynamics of a Life of Renunciation', in *New Horizons of Indian Christian Living*, ed. S. Chackalackal, Bengaluru: Vidyavanam.

Trafford, P. (2016) *Fuengsin's Life and Work*, accessible on http://fuengsin.org/

—— (2016a) *Thursday's Lotus: The Life and Work of Fuengsin Trafford*. London: CreateSpace.

Tyler, P. M. (1997) *The Way of Ecstasy: Praying with Teresa of Avila*. Norwich: Canterbury Press.

—— (2000) 'Thomas Merton: Ikon of Commitment for the Postmodern Generation', *The Way Supplement*, 2000/98.

—— (2011) *The Return to the Mystical: Ludwig Wittgenstein, Teresa of Avila and the Christian Mystical Tradition*. London: Continuum.

—— (2013) *Teresa of Avila: Doctor of the Soul*. London: Bloomsbury.

—— (2016) *The Pursuit of the Soul: Psychoanalysis, Soul-making and the Christian Tradition*. Edinburgh: T&T Clark.

—— (2017) 'Mystical affinities: St Teresa and Jean Gerson', in *Teresa of Avila: Mystical Theology and Spirituality in the Carmelite Tradition*, ed. P. M. Tyler and E. Howells. London: Routledge, pp. 36–51.

—— (2017a) *Confession: The Healing of the Soul*. London: Bloomsbury.

—— (forthcoming) 'Mystical Desire: St Ignatius of Loyola and Affective Dionysianism', in *Id Quod Volo: The Dynamics of Desire in the Spiritual Exercises and Postmodernity*, ed. J. Hanvey and T. La Couter. Leiden: Brill.

—— (forthcoming) 'The Carthusians and the *Cloud of Unknowing*', in *The Oxford Handbook to Dionysius the Areopagite*, ed. M. Edwards, D. Pallis and G. Steiris. Oxford: Oxford University Press.

Tyler, P. M. and E. Howells, eds (2017) *Teresa of Avila: Mystical Theology and Spirituality in the Carmelite Tradition*. London: Routledge.

von Balthasar, H. U. (1961–9) *Herrlichkeit: Eine theologische Ästhetik*, trans. 'The Glory of the Lord: A Theological Aesthetic' (1982–9), ed. J. Fessio and J. Riches, trans. O. Davies, A. Louth, J. Sayward, M. Simon, B. McNeil, F. McDonagh, J. Riches, E. Leiva-Merikakis and R. Williams. Edinburgh: T&T Clark.

Ward, B., ed. (1984) *The Sayings of the Desert Fathers*. Kalamazoo, MI: Cistercian Publications.

Welch, J. (1982) *Spiritual Pilgrims: Carl Jung and Teresa of Avila*. New York: Paulist.

White, C., trans. (1998) *Early Christian Lives*. London: Penguin.

Žižek, S. (2001) 'From Western Marxism to Western Buddhism', published online at *Cabinet* http://www.cabinetmagazine.org/issues/2/western.php

Church documents and Scripture

The Documents of Vatican II, ed. W. Abbott. London: Geoffrey Chapman, 1966.

Christian and Jewish Scripture Quotations from the *New Revised Standard Version*, London: Harper, 2007 with modifications as necessary.

Hindu Scripture Quotations from *Hindu Scriptures*, trans. R. C. Zaehner, London: Dent, 1966 with modifications as necessary.

Buddhist Scripture Quotations from *The Middle Length Discourses of the Buddha*, trans. Bhikkhu Nāṇamoli and Bhikkhu Bodhi, Oxford: Pali Text Society, 2002, and *The Connected Discourses of the Buddha*, trans. Bhikkhu Bodhi, Somerville: Wisdom, 2000 with modifications as necessary.

Index of Names and Subjects

Abhishktananda 142
Acharya, Francis 142
Aesthetical Discourses (Isaiah of Scetis) 21
agnosticism, mindfulness and 3
Anālayo 8
Andrés Martín, Melquíades 39–40
anger 21
St Anthony 20
　demons and the Psalms 22
　enjoyment and 23
Aquinas, St Thomas 80
　habits of virtue 130
Ascent of Mount Carmel (John of the Cross) 79–85
ātāpi 8
St Athanasius
　biography of Anthony 20
St Augustine of Hippo 71
　Spanish printings of 40
The Awakening of the Spring (Tagore) 124–5
Aziz, Abdul 101

Balma, Hugh of
　Cisneros and 45–6

Viae Sion Lugent 42, 44
Balthasar, Hans Urs von 79, 109
Bashô 118
Bays, Chozen 2, 3
St Benedict
　Rule for Beginners 23, 24
St Bernard 40
Bernini, Gian Lorenzo
　Ecstasy of Saint Teresa 63
Bhikku Bhodi 9, 10
Blake, William 96
The Bliss of the Lord exercise 146–9
body scan exercises 35–7
St Bonaventure
　Cisneros and 42
　Hopkins and 93
Book of the Life (Teresa of Avila) 51–4, 62–3
Buddhism
　bonds of *dukkha* 32
　Buddha's scepticism 3
　Christian prayer and 28, 30–1
　dialogue with Christianity 7
　influence on Merton 104–9

mantras 89
Merton and 98, 100, 114, 119
mindfulness and 8–10, viii–ix
'monkey mind' 52
sati 41, 44, 153
Spanish mystical writers 41, 55
Trafford teaches *Dhamma* 5–7
Zen 104–9, 114

Carmelites 18
Carretto, Carlo 18
Cassian, John 103, 153
  Conferences 23, 27–8, 30–3, 115
  extremes meet 69
  four modes of prayer 31–2
  ordinary life and prayer 64–5
  purity of heart 27–8, 115–17
Catholic Worker Movement 99
Chadwick, Bishop Graham vii
chakras/wheels 147–9
Chapters on Prayer (Evagrius) 20–1
Christianity
  ascetics 143–4
  Buddhism and 7, ix
  early desert tradition 17–19
  Orthodox Jesus prayer 88–9
  tradition of mindfulness 153–4
  transcendental 28–9
Chryssavgis, John
  Heart of the Desert 27
Cisneros, García Jiménez de
  Balma and Dionysius 45–6, 47
  Directorio de las Horas Canónicas 42
  Spiritual Exercises 40, 41–4, 54–5
  Teresa of Avila and 50
Cistercians 92
St Clare 67
Clément, O., on prayer 29–30
Climate of Monastic Prayer (Merton) 101
The Cloud of Unknowing 55
cognitive therapy, mindfulness-based 2
Coincidentia Oppositorium (de Cusa) 135, 136
Conférences (Cassian) 23, 115
  mindfulness and prayer 30–3
  prayerfulness 27–8
Confession: The Healing of the Soul (Tyler) 126
Constantine the Great, Emperor 19
'Contemplation to Attain Love' exercise 154–7
Contemplative Prayer (Merton) 120

INDEX OF NAMES AND SUBJECTS

Coptic Cycle of Sayings
  (Pseudo-Macarius) 88
Corinthians, Second Letter to
  13.5 22
Cullen, Chris 35
Cusa, Nicholas de
  Coincidentia Oppositorium
  135, 136

Dalai Lama (Fourteenth) 119
The Dark Night of the Soul
  (John of the Cross) 79, 80,
  144
Davids, Thomas William
  Rhys 8
D'Costa, Gavin ix
demons and passions
  Evagrius on 20–1
  noonday 25–6
  seven types of 21–2
desert tradition
  body scan exercises 35–7
  emergence of Christianity
    17–19
  fathers and mothers of
    19–23, 34–5
  mindfulness and 28–34
  physical and psychological
    34
  tourists in 24
  what monks do 20–3
desires *see* demons and
  passions
Dhamma
  Buddhist context of 9
  Trafford teaches 5–7
St Dionysius 45–6

Directorio de las Horas
  Canónicas (Cisneros) 42
dying, mindful end and 144–6

Ecstasy of Saint Teresa
  (Bernini) 63
education, *Brahmacarya* and
  129–30
Eiximenis, Francesc
  Tractat de contemplació 42
'Endless Death' (Tagore)
  145–6
environment, Merton and
  108–10
envy 21
Evagrius of Pontus
  acedia/noonday demon
    25–6
  Chapters on Prayer 20–1
  the Jesus prayer 88
  Praktikos 20–1
  On Prayer 29
excess 69
exercises
  The Bliss of the Lord 146–9
  body scan 35–7
  'Contemplation to Attain
    Love' 154–7
  One-pointed Heart
    Devotion 120–2
  Prayer of the Name 87–9
  the raisin 14
  sacred breath 56–7
  silence 11–14
Exodus, Book of
  3 17
  19 17

Faith and Violence (Merton) 113
Feniger, Siegmund (Nyanponika Thera) 9
Finley, James 26–7
Forest, Jim 98
fourfold path
  Brahmacarya (education) 129–30
  Gṛhasta (middle life) 131–7
  mid-life 133–7
  Sannyāsa (renunciation) 140–4
  Tagore's lectures and 128–9
  Vānaprastha (loosening bonds) 137–40
Fowler, James 133–4, 140, 145
St Francis of Assisi 140
Francis, Pope 141, 144
Franciscans, Merton and 97
Frederic, Dom, Abbott 98
Freud, Sigmund 145
  desert spirituality and 19
  the passions and 21, 22
Friends of the Western Buddhist Order, Bethnal Green 6

Gaew, Ajahn 5
Galatians, First Letter to 18
Ganeri, Fr Martin, OP ix
Genesis, Book of
  2.7 56
Gerson, Jean 42, 44
Gethin, Rupert 55
Gethsemani Abbey *see* Our Lady of Gethsemani Abbey
Gibson, Étienne
  The Spirit of Medieval Philosophy 96
Giroux, Robert 98
God
  meditating on images of 79–82
  Merton's eye and 108–12
  passions and 21
  see also Jesus Christ
Grail question 127–8, 139, 140
  in the Castle 126–7, 134, 136–7
Grayston, D. 101
greed 21
Gregory Nazianzen 21
Griffiths, Bede 142

Hahn, Thich Nhat 65
Hall, Sr Mary 4
The Heart of Buddhist Meditation (Nyanponika Thera) 9
Heart of the Desert (Chryssavgis) 27
Heelas, Paul 1
Hesse, Herman 140, 144
hesychia see silence/*hesychia*
Hinduism
  mantras 89
  Merton and 98, 100
  see also Indian tradition
Hopkins, Gerard Manley
  Merton and 93, 96, 108, 109

INDEX OF NAMES AND SUBJECTS

Hosea
  2.14 17

The Idea of the Holy
  (Otto) 126
St Ignatius of Loyola 42
  method with scripture
    121–2
  Spiritual Exercises 49,
    154–7
Indian traditions
  aspects of breath 57
  chakras/wheels 147–9
  fourfold stages of life
    128–44
  transcendental tradition
    123–8
  see also Buddhism;
    Hinduism
intercession, Cassian on 31,
  32
The Interior Castle (Teresa
  of Avila) 51–2, 76, 86–7,
  133–4, 140, 146, 156
Isaac of Nineveh 11
  person becomes prayer 33
  on silence 13
Isaiah of Scetis
  Aesthetical Discourses 21
Islam
  images of God and 79
  Sufism 89, 114

jealousy 21
Jeevan Dhara ashram 141,
  143
Jenkins, Ruth 93

Jesus Christ
  divine reading of 120–2
  healing 147, 148–9
  as ikon of God 78, 79
  John and the desert 18
  Lord's Prayer and 73–4, 77
  mindfulness of 71–6
  Orthodox Jesus prayer
    88–9
  the Passion of 32–3
John, Gospel of
  20.19–22 57, 121
St John of the Cross 71, 141
  Ascent of Mount Carmel
    79–85
  The Dark Night of the Soul
    79, 80, 144–5
  influence on Merton 102
  meditation on images of
    God 79–82
  places of meditation 82–5
  Teresa of Avila and 85–6
St John the Baptist 17–18
John XXIII, Pope St 100
Johnson, Robert
  Grail question 127
  meaning and 137
  on the middle years 131, 136
Joyce, James 35
Judaism
  desert tradition and 17
  Hasidism 114
  images of God and 79
Jung, Carl G. 13, 145
  desert spirituality and 19
  gold in the wilderness 24
  The Stages of Life 134–5

171

Kabat-Zinn, Jon 53
    MBSR programme 1–3
    the raisin exercise 14
kairos, Merton and 117–18
Kempf, Nicholas 42
Kempis, Thomas à 42
Kochumuttom, Fr Thomas, CMI 141, 142–3
Kornfield, John 65, 132

Laws of Manu 129, 132
Leahy, G. F. 96
LeClerq, Jean 115
'Letter to an Activist' (Merton) 113–14
Levinson, D. 140
The Life of St Anthony (Athanasius) 21, 22
Little Brothers and Sisters of Jesus 18
Lord's Prayer 33
Loyola *see* St Ignatius of Loyola
Ludoph of Saxony
    Vita Christi 42
Luis de Léon, Fray 63
Luke, Gospel of
    9.33 81
lust 21

Macarius, Abba, the Jesus prayer and 88
McCabe, Herbert 27
Mace, C. 2–4
Mark, Gospel of
    Mark 1 17
'Marxism and Monastic Perspectives' (Merton) 119

material world, St Teresa and 64–70
Matthew, Gospel of
    4 18
meditation *see* prayer and meditation
Mello, Anthony de SJ 11, 12
Merton, John Paul 94
Merton, Owen 93, 94–5
Merton, Thomas
    Buddhism and 119
    clarity and 114–18, 153
    contemplation and 100–4
    death of 118–19
    early life 92–7
    entrance to life as monk 96–8
    Hindu and Buddhist influences 98, 100
    kairos 117
    late love 110–11
    lectures 114–18
    mindful eye of 107–12
    on silence 11
    social engagement 112–14, 132, 139
    Zen and 104–9
    works of
        Climate of Monastic Prayer 101
        Contemplative Prayer 120
        Faith and Violence 113
        'Letter to an Activist' 113–14
        'Marxism and Monastic Perspectives' 119

New Seeds of Contemplation 104, 106, 109, 118
Seeds of Contemplation 100–4
The Seven Storey Mountain 92–8, 113
Sign of Jonas 97
Zen and the Birds of Appetite 104, 111, 116
Merton (Thomas) Foundation 114
mindfulness
 agnosticism and 3
 Buddhist concepts and 8–10, viii–ix
 of Christ 71–6
 in Christian tradition 153–4
 contemporary interest in 1–4, viii
 desert tradition and 28–34
 Dhamma training 5–7
 dying and 144–6
 exercises ix–x
 habit of 130
 'heartfulness' 3, 10
 larger sense of self and 135–7
 Merton and 100–4, 116–18
 oración mental 46–50, 51–5, 70–2, 76–7, 82, 85–6
 Palma and 46–50
 Teresa of Avila and 52–4, 65–78
 as therapy 2–3
 training in 4–7

see also prayer and meditation; silence
Mindfulness-Based Cognitive Therapy 2, 47
Mindfulness-Based Stress Reduction 2, 47
Mombaer, Jan 42
Monchanin, Jules 142
monks
 derivation of term 19
 noonday demons 25–6
 what they do in the desert 20–3
Montserrat, Abbey of 40, 41–2
My Reminiscences (Tagore) 123–4

neo-Platonism and the soul 31
New Seeds of Contemplation (Merton) 104, 106, 109, 118
nothingness, Palma's *Nada* and 50
the numinous, encountering 125
Nyanponika Thera (Siegmund Feniger) *The Heart of Buddhist Meditation* 9

Obras de Bonaventura 40
On Prayer (Evagrius of Pontus) 29
On Prayer (Origen) 29
One-pointed Heart Devotion exercise 120–2

oración mental 76–7, 82, 85–6
  Palme and 46–50
  Teresa of Avila and 51–5, 70–2
Origen
  On Prayer 29
Osuna, Francisco de
  material and spiritual 68
  Teresa of Avila and 44, 50
  The Third Spiritual Alphabet 29, 40, 50–1
Otto, Rudolf
  The Idea of the Holy 126
Our Lady of Gethsemani Abbey
  Merton and 92, 97, 100, 119

Palma, Bernabé de
  oración mental 46–50
  The Spiritual Way 47–9
Pattathu, Paul 142
St Paul
  the body as the Temple 35
  Christ as ikon of God 78, 79
  in the desert 18
  examine and test yourself 22
  prayers for everyone 31
  Trinitarian shape of prayer vii
Peace in the Post-Christian Era (Merton) 99
Perumpallikunnel, Kurian, CMI 141

St Peter 81
Phaedrus (Plato) 21
places of prayer 82–5
Plato
  Phaedrus 21
pleasures, Evagrius on 21
Poemen, Abba
  on demons 22
  on evil thoughts 24
  on excess 69
  on silence 26
Praktikos (Evagrius) 20–1
  on the noonday demon 25–6
Prasanna Devi 141
prayer and meditation
  Christian mindfulness 153–4
  daily life and 64–5
  four modes of 32–3
  of the heart 28, 30
  on images of God 79–82
  Lord's 33, 73–4, 77
  Orthodox Jesus prayer 88–9
  places of 82–5
  prayerfulness 27–8
  tranquility 30
  transcendent 28–9, 33–4, ix
  Trinitarian shape of vii
  using images and 79–82
Prayer of the Name exercise 87–9
Pseudo-Macarius
  Coptic Cycle of Sayings 88
psychology, Merton's interest in 114

INDEX OF NAMES AND SUBJECTS

The Pursuit of the Soul
  (Tyler) 126, 135
raisin exercise 14
Rani Maria, Sr 144
recogimiento 40, 47, 50,
  53–4, 75
The Religion of Man
  (Tagore) 139–40
  the fourfold stages of life
  128–44
Richard of St Victor 40
The Robin 1
Roman Catholic Church
  Merton's conversion 96–7
  Trafford's comment on 6–7
Romans, Letter to
  8.26–29 vii
Rule for Beginners (St
  Benedict) 23, 24

sacred breath exercise 56–7
Sadanand, Swami 141,
  143–4
Sarayutpilag, Fuengsilapa *see*
  Trafford, Fuengsin
sati 153
  Spanish mysticism and 41,
  44
Satipaṭṭhana Sutta 8
Saux, Henri le 142
Sayādaw, Mahāsī 9
*Sayings of the Desert
  Fathers and Mothers/
  Apophthegmata* 20
Scharf, Robert 9
Seeds of Contemplation
  (Merton) 100–4

Selly Oak Colleges,
  Birmingham University 4
The Seven Storey Mountain
  (Merton) 113
  entrance to life as monk
  96–8
  on Merton's early life
  92–7
  writing and publication of
  97–8
sexual desire, twisting of
  21–2
Shakespeare, William 145
Shapiro, S. 3
Sign of Jonas (Merton) 97
silence/*hesychia*
  exercises in 11–14
  of the heart 26–8
sloth 21
Smith, Christine vii
social engagement 112–14,
  132, 139
Society of Jesus mindfulness
  training 4
soul, discourse about 126
Spain
  Cisneros and 40, 41–4,
  41–6
  'Golden Age' of mystical
  writing 39–41
  St John of the Cross 79–85
  Palma's *oración mental*
  46–50
  recogimiento 40, 47, 50,
  53–4, 75
  riches and honour 68
  Teresa of Avila and 51–5

175

see also St Ignatius of
  Loyola; St John of the
  Cross; St Teresa of Avila
The Spirit of Medieval
  Philosophy (Gibson) 96
Spiritual Exercises (Cisneros)
  40, 41–4, 54–5
Spiritual Exercises (Ignatius
  of Loyola) 49
  'Contemplation to Attain
    Love' 154–7
The Spiritual Way (Palma)
  47–9
Sri Aurobindo 57
The Stages of Life (Jung)
  134–5
Sufism, music and 89
supplication, Cassian on 31
Suzuki, D. T. 104
Syncletica, Amma 24

Tagore, Debendranath
  138–9
Tagore, Rabindranath
  awakening experience
    123–6
  the fourfold stages of life
    128–44
  on Western approach
    137–8
  works of
    The Awakening of the
      Spring 124–5
    Endless Death 145–6
    My Reminiscences 123–4
    The Religion of Man 128,
      139–40

St Teresa of Avila
  on being human 35
  Christ and mindfulness
    71–6
  context of writings 61–4
  the divine in the pots and
    pans 136
  images of God 79
  influences on 46, 50–1
  John of the Cross and 85–6
  life as a bad inn 154
  'little deserts' 18
  Lord's Prayer and 73–4, 77
  Merton and 116, 117
  mindfulness/*oración mental*
    51–5, 70–2, 76–7, 82,
    85–6
  Osuna and 40, 44, 50–1
  social engagement of 132,
    139
  works of
    Book of the Life 51–4,
      62–3
    The Interior Castle 14, 76,
      86–7, 133–4, 140, 146,
      156
    The Way of Perfection 55,
      61, 64–78, 79, 85
  the world in flames 66–7
Thanissaro Bhikku 8
thanksgiving, Cassian on 31,
  32
The Third Spiritual Alphabet
  (de Osuna) 29, 50–1
Thottakara, A. 132, 143
Timothy, First Letter to
  2.1 31

INDEX OF NAMES AND SUBJECTS

Tomlinson, Ian SJ 4
Tractat de contemplació (Eiximenis) 42
Trafford, Fuengsin 4–7
Trafford, Paul 4–5
Trafford, Tony 4
tranquility, prayer and 30
Trappists *see* Merton, Thomas; Our Lady of Gesthemani Abbey
Tyler, Peter
  Confession 126
  The Pursuit of the Soul 126, 135
  The Way of Ecstasy viii

Upanishads 126
  four stages of life 129
  Tagore's father and 138

Vedas 126
Viae Sion Lugent (Balma) 42, 44
Vineeth, Fr Francis, CMI 7, 143

Ward, Sr Benedicta 20
The Way of Ecstasy - Praying with St Teresa of Avila (Tyler) viii
The Way of Perfection (Teresa of Avila) 55, 61, 85
  preparation and disposition 64–70
Weil, Simone 101
Welch, Jack, OCD 133–4
Williams, Mark 2
wisdom, divine unknowing 102, 103
Woodhead, Linda 1

yoga ix

Zen and the Birds of Appetite (Merton) 104, 111, 116
Zen Buddhism, Merton and 104–9
Žižek, Slavoj 66
Zutfen, Gérard Zerbolt de 42